Business Perspective 2
The Business View on Successful
IT Service Delivery

 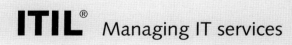

London: TSO

Published by TSO (The Stationery Office) and available from:

Online
www.tsoshop.co.uk

Mail, Telephone, Fax & E-mail
TSO
PO Box 29, Norwich, NR3 1GN
Telephone orders/General enquiries: 0870 600 5522
Fax orders: 0870 600 5533
E-mail: customer.services@tso.co.uk
Textphone 0870 240 3701

TSO Shops
123 Kingsway, London, WC2B 6PQ
020 7242 6393 Fax 020 7242 6394
16 Arthur Street, Belfast BT1 4GD
028 9023 8451 Fax 028 9023 5401
71 Lothian Road, Edinburgh EH3 9AZ
0870 606 5566 Fax 0870 606 5588

TSO@Blackwell and other Accredited Agents

For further information on OGC products, contact:

OGC Service Desk
Rosebery Court
St Andrews Business Park
Norwich NR7 0HS

Telephone +44 (0) 845 000 4999

First published 2006

ISBN-10 0 11 330969 4
ISBN-13 978 011 330969 6

Printed in the United Kingdom for The Stationery Office

CONTENTS

ACKNOWLEDGEMENTS

Authors

The guidance in this book was distilled from the experience of a range of authors working in IT Service Management. The material was written by:

Pippa Bass	OGC
Tony Betts	OGC
Fatima Cabral	Pink Elephant
Jane Chittenden	Format Publishing
Jenny Dugmore	Service Matters
Rubina Faber	Regal Training Ltd
Isabel Feher-Watters	Pink Elephant
David Hinley	Enodatum Ltd
Steve Ingall	Fox IT
Brian Johnson	CA
Mike Linsdell	TSO
Peter Musgrave	Reccan Ltd
Christopher Ouellette	BearingPoint
Parmjit Sangha	Quint Wellington Redwood
Porter Sherman	UBS Investment Bank
Cheryl E. Simpson	Independent
Rob Stroud	CA
Arnold van Mameren	Getronics
Deborah Wagner	BearingPoint

Editors

Jane Chittenden	Format Publishing
Brian Johnson	CA

Reviewers

A wide-ranging national and international quality assurance (QA) exercise was carried out by people proposed by TSO, OGC and *it*SMF. TSO, OGC and *it*SMF wish to express their particular appreciation to the following people who spent considerable time and effort on QA of the material.

Tony Betts	OGC
Gordon Brown	Plexent
Alison Cartlidge	Xansa
Jane Chittenden	Format Publishing
Jim Clinch	OGC
Lynda Cooper	Fox IT
Graham Dawson	HP
Irene Driveklepp	Teleplan AS
Jenny Dugmore	Service Matters
Kevin Ellis	Bank of Montreal Financial Group
John Gibert	Southcourt Ltd
Gerry Gough	HP
John Groom	West Groom Consulting
David Hinley	Enodatum Ltd
Carl Howard	Plexent
Steve Ingall	Fox IT
Majid Iqbal	Carnegie Mellon University
Shirley Lacy	Connectsphere
Gerry McLaughlin	Fox IT
Colin Mayers	Mayers Consulting Ltd
Ron Muns	HDI
Peter Musgrave	Reccan Ltd
Bruce Pinnington	Essential CS
Vera Rodrigues	Fujitsu Services
Frances Scarff	OGC
John Windebank	Sun Microsystems

I INTRODUCTION

I.I Overview

Best practice and standards-based approaches have an important role to play in the management of IT. This book sets the business's IT capability in the context of OGC's IT Infrastructure Library (ITIL), the most widely accepted approach to IT Service Management in the world. It is a key enabler in ensuring that IT service providers deliver services with the reliability, availability and security to meet the demands of today's business.

The ITIL volume *Business Perspective: The IS View on Delivering Services to the Business* was published in 2004. Its purpose was to explain to IT service suppliers how to engage more effectively with their business customers. The primary target audience was the customer relationship manager in the supplier organisation. This is the companion volume, *Business Perspective 2*, which brings together key messages about IT written for the business by experts in their field. It focuses on what Management Boards need to know to ensure that they have appropriate IT capability for their organisations.

This volume consists of a set of papers on key topics on aligning the business and IT; they are written by leading IT experts and draw on internationally recognised research. The papers are not written in the form of detailed ITIL practices since this would vastly extend the scope of ITIL. It deliberately leaves open a much wider range of forms of alignment of IT services with the wider organisation.

This chapter provides an overview of the main themes of the book, together with a brief context-setting outline; this explains why IT is critical to the business, given the complexity of the modern organisation's business relationships.

I.2 Why IT is a critical business issue

The importance of IT to business success has grown significantly in recent years. Today, organisations use IT to transform their business by restructuring internal functions, redesigning interfaces to other organisations and introducing information-based business activities that did not exist previously. Many of these developments depend on the exploitation of communication facilities and the applications that use them, such as e-mail and the Internet, groupware and information-supply services. Businesses and public sector bodies are using IT to link users within the organisation and with their customers and other external bodies, and to exploit the potential of shared information.

Modern businesses will use IT to support their key relationships with partners, suppliers and their delivery chains – not necessarily a simple interface between external customers, the business and its suppliers. They may also need to take account of global dimensions if trading internationally or as part of a global enterprise.

IT is a business issue just as much as a technology issue. Strategic management of information and IT is an important part of the Management Board's role. It is essential for ensuring that IT is fully exploited to the benefit of the organisation. The potential benefits are:

- simplified and automated processes, tasks and transactions to increase speed, reduce costs and improve productivity and quality

- enhanced decision-making at all levels by providing better quality data and information that is more relevant and more timely, delivered to the right people at the right time

- improved integration of employees and customers by connecting them in new ways over large geographic areas and organisational boundaries.

1.3   Overview of the chapters in this guide

Chapter 2: Corporate strategy and IT

As a member of the Board you need to know that your **corporate strategy** includes planning for your IT requirements to meet your main business objectives. Chapter 2 describes how to set and manage the strategic direction for the business, of which IT is a part, along with information, finance and human resources (HR). It explains why it is critically important for the business to own and lead its corporate strategy.

This chapter describes how corporate strategy defines the context for the business's IT capability, its services and governance. Where IT is an important contributor to business performance, it will need to be integrated with corporate strategy. Where it plays more of a supporting role, decisions about IT are likely to be delegated to individual business areas and managed via a corporate IT strategy that focuses specifically on issues such as interoperability (enabling the organisation to work coherently within its organisational boundaries and outside with partners), data sharing and data protection.

Chapter 3: IT governance

You must be confident that the **governance** arrangements in your organisation are robust enough to stand up to scrutiny; part of that governance is IT governance (Chapter 3). It describes the key components of an IT governance framework, how the business leads on governance and owns it; and how the various parties report to the business.

Corporate governance is being significantly tightened in most organisations in response to external regulation by governments and international bodies (exemplified by the Sarbanes-Oxley Act and Basel II).

Effective governance of the business's IT capability ensures that major decisions about investment in IT are made on the basis of their contribution to business objectives. Chapter 3 describes two prominent sources of IT governance advice: work by the MIT Sloan School of Management Center for Information Systems Research and the IT Governance Institute CobiT® *Control Objectives for Information and related Technology* framework. However the governance of IT is organised, senior representatives of business units should make the key investment decisions.

Effective IT governance achieves the following key benefits:

- better control over IT costs, risks and resources
- compliance with statutory requirements of external regulators and other stakeholders by harnessing IT to automate processes and controls, assess control effectiveness, manage compliance activities from concept through production, and provide reliable audit trails
- alignment with business objectives and improved value for the business.

Chapter 4: Managing change

Your organisation will have programmes of **change** throughout its life – perhaps introducing new business services or changing working practices. IT will be a major enabler of change, so you need to be sure that IT-enabled change is managed well in your organisation. Chapter 4 explains that the business must be proactive about change, not just reactive. It describes the drivers and forces for change, together with practical advice on making change 'stick'.

This chapter also looks at the issue of controlling changes to the IT infrastructure and services in the context of managing business change. The increasingly pervasive influence of IT, supporting (or potentially inhibiting) changes in business direction and performance, requires a flexible IT infrastructure and services that are able to adapt to a changing environment. The chapter highlights the interaction between the ITIL processes – Release Management, Change Management, Configuration Management and Service Level Management – and how these need to be aligned with other corporate Change Management processes, including project and programme management.

Chapter 5: Business and service continuity

You will be at risk of going out of business if your IT systems and services are inadequate or fail, and there is no **business continuity** arrangement to keep you going until normal service is restored. You need to be sure that business continuity plans are robust. Chapter 5 helps to ensure that the organisation is always able to cope with the unexpected, recover from disasters, etc. – in short, providing confidence about continuity of service whatever is ahead.

This chapter looks at the demands on modern organisations for continuous IT service provision. It highlights the potential trade-off between the demand for flexibility and speed in IT service and the increasing need for availability and security. Given the increasing dependency of organisations on IT, it is increasingly important that senior managers decide the way in which continuity is ensured by developing continuity plans, testing them and maintaining them. The options for recovery of the online customer service are an inherent part of the overall business service.

Business continuity is no longer solely about protecting the organisation's own assets, ring-fenced from third parties. In networked organisations, information flows across organisational boundaries. The modern era of collaborative working styles, selective partnerships and outsourcing means that the organisation's security and business continuity measures are far more wide-reaching: they do not affect just one company, but possibly hundreds. If partners and suppliers cease to operate, for even the shortest time, it has an impact throughout the entire extended enterprise.

Chapter 6: IT asset management

You are accountable for your organisation's assets, which include IT. You therefore need to be able to account for the **IT assets**. Chapter 6 describes how to ensure that the business understands the value delivered by its IT, its IT requirements, how to obtain them and how to manage them.

IT asset management is about optimising the use and control of IT assets and mitigating related risks. It is important in enabling the organisation to meet its fiduciary, legal and regulatory obligations.

IT asset management tracks and monitors the organisation's IT assets; it is a powerful tool for controlling costs and avoiding unnecessary expenditure. It also enables the organisation to assess how well its IT is aligned to current and future business needs.

New ways of working in which individuals are mobile or work remotely, perhaps from home, add to the complexity of managing assets. Where organisations collaborate to deliver services their IT systems become increasingly interdependent. Assets need to be managed to a common standard to support the network as a whole.

Chapter 7: Sourcing of IT services

You will have to make decisions about **sourcing**, going out to the IT services industry from time to time to obtain IT services, acquire new IT or update what you have. You need to be confident that you are getting good value for money and the best source of supply for your IT needs. Chapter 7 explains how to make informed choices about acquiring and managing IT services from external sources.

There are a variety of reasons that may drive an organisation to seek the delivery of IT services from third parties. These include reducing costs, increasing organisational focus, obtaining expertise, sharing risk, accelerating change and so on. A major concern from a business perspective should be the retention of service and contract management capability within the organisation. Adoption of ITIL may be a precursor to outsourcing, providing a stable and known reference point against which to judge potential improvements from outsourcing. ITIL should be a contractual requirement of IT service providers and may form the basis of integration where multiple service providers are working together to deliver end-to-end service.

A more strategic view of IT seeks to identify an IT services partner to deliver benefits for the business. The procurement of a partner must comply with legal constraints, but must emphasise shared vision, trust and value for money. The key requirement is the degree to which the partner should add value in terms of knowledge flows to the relationship and not simply provide IT capability.

Understanding the relationship that arises in IT service contracts (including outsourcing) is critical, since it comes about not only through implementing the contract, but also as a natural consequence of the resulting issue of dependency.

Chapter 8: Knowledge management

Your organisation depends on its corporate **knowledge**. Chapter 8 describes how to manage the organisation's business information. It takes account of people issues: cultural and behavioural aspects; process issues; technology issues.

This chapter emphasises that understanding knowledge and information flows is essential to successful exploitation of IT. There is no single definition of knowledge management but the term generally refers to capturing the knowledge of individuals so that this knowledge becomes available as an organisational resource. In this way, the organisation dependent on knowledge for its competitive advantage is less susceptible to people 'walking out of the door' with this key asset.

One of the main factors in redesigning customer-facing processes is the way in which knowledge about customers is coordinated. Bringing together different sets of data about a customer into a single customer view not only enables considerable reduction in costs but is also at the heart of effective online service. An important consideration, especially where IT services are shared, is the privacy and confidentiality of customer information.

When organisations are stretched across time and space, and restructured around virtual teams and networks, opportunities for the sharing of knowledge and learning based on physical proximity and specialisation are lost. Corporate management of business knowledge storage and transfer using IT becomes essential.

Chapter 9: Standards and best practice

Finally, you need to be aware of the relevant **standards** and best practice underpinning all of these management topics. Chapter 9 explains how to put these principles into practice. It provides practical advice on selecting best practice and standards-based approaches in creating a governance framework for managing IT effectively.

Standards and best practice can provide evidence that you have managed things appropriately in the event of (say) a disaster. More importantly, they enable you to work consistently with many different suppliers; they save money because you can standardise components and be sure they all fit together (interoperability); they give you confidence that things are delivered to an agreed and verifiable quality.

In the extended enterprise, members of the network may enjoy considerable degrees of independence and there may be no clear-cut hierarchy to resolve conflicts. In this type of organisational context, strict adherence to external standards for communication becomes extremely important. ITIL helps to ensure that the IT infrastructure and IT services provide effective, coherent support for the way the business wishes to operate with other stakeholders to deliver to customers. ITIL is an important part of the picture but there are other standards and best practice that can be integrated depending on business needs.

There is no framework of standards and best practice for a given organisation. The reality is that every organisation must face the challenge of defining its own framework and targeting those standards and best practice approaches that uniquely address the organisation's culture, mission and internal policies. To evaluate the potential contribution of a standard or best practice approach, the chapter advocates evaluating them against:

- a vision for IT Service Management (ITSM) – the desired end-state you want to achieve
- a strategy for achieving the ITSM vision – requirements and methods necessary to achieve the vision
- an ITSM implementation roadmap – a high-level plan indicating the steps and relative sequencing to achieve the vision.

Chapter 10: Bibliography and further information

The Bibliography contains details of the information sources cited in the text.

Appendices

The appendices to the guide provide more detailed information about standards and best practice, including references to OGC's approaches for managing programmes, projects and risk. There is also a glossary of terms used.

2 CORPORATE STRATEGY AND IT

2.1 Key messages for the Board

Corporate strategy must ensure that the business and IT strategies are aligned. In today's fast-moving business and technical environment it is essential that the organisation's IT is flexible and agile enough to respond to change. There must also be leadership in IT, continued senior management commitment to change, well-managed approaches to risk and the capability for the organisation to learn from experience.

2.2 Overview

Radical changes to the business may be helped or hampered by the extent to which attention is being paid to IT issues. Business managers will be more than familiar with creation of corporate strategy; the intention of the following is not to suggest that IT can strategise more creatively but to draw attention to the special attention needed when IT is integral to drive (often radical) change in business. IT is often (quite properly) relegated to being a commodity purchase; the procurement of IT should be no different from the procurement of other major services. The way in which IT is used and deployed, however, needs proper consideration to maximise effectiveness.

2.3 What is radical change?

Within a business context, radical change can be defined as change that has a high impact on the business organisation and is carried out over a fairly short period of time, typically less than a year. And typically, IT will be used to drive changes.

High impact changes affect:

- the scope of an organisation: choosing to provide to an entirely new type of customer, or the organisation being sold. Examples of this type of change are privatisation (new owners, new customer approach) and management buy-outs (new owners)
- the structure of an organisation: changing the organisation's hierarchy and management controls by means of a thorough reorganisation, merger or acquisition
- the core process of an organisation: for instance, an airline company that takes on the challenge to fulfil all transportation needs, whether by air, land or sea.

2.4   IT as a business resource

What is this IT capability?

The box in the computer room?
My secretary's PC?
The label printer in packaging?
Standalone PCs?
Embedded electronics?
The copying machine?

The electronic mail system?
That overview from production?
The graphics from sales?
The customer database?
The payments tape?
The computer department manager?
The guy who fixes the printer?

That report on electronic data interchange?
The manual for our project control system?
The training organised for our new personnel system?
How my assistant puts financial results in my monthly report?
The quarterly meeting with those software people?
The phone number I dial when my PC doesn't work?
That computer supplier I met last week?

Figure 2.1 – IT capability

It is apparent that IT must be dealt with in some way or another. But what is it? It is not IT in isolation, nor is it merely the central IT department. It has to do with the way in which IT is used and organised. In effect, it is the IT capability: the ability of the organisation to make best use of the benefits that IT can offer.

One of the first actions is to determine what it is and what it does in your particular organisation. Figure 2.1 suggests the questions to ask. Try to create a mental image of what the IT capability is in terms of:

- equipment involved in the processing, storage and transfer of data and information, such as computers, calculators, telephones and faxes, printers, terminals, etc.

- the way in which this equipment is all linked together, perhaps crossing national and continental borders

- the software that enables the machinery to perform its automated functions and which establishes links between otherwise unintelligent machines

- the applications that make it possible for people to perform specific tasks

- all the functions and processes in your organisation provided by or supported through the use of IT

- the people who handle operational tasks, and the people who possess the know-how to plan, expand and change the IT capability, or parts of it: how do they work together, and what is their place in the organisation as a whole?

- the methods and techniques used to plan, change and control the organisation's IT capability. Does the organisation know and learn how to use IT in the most effective manner?

- the formal organisation of the IT capability: its structure, procedures, the reward system.

Most organisations depend on IT in order to prosper. This is why IT should be considered as a factor in the corporate strategy process, just like other resources such as people, money, office space, raw materials, equipment, etc. An inadequate provision of any of these resources, either during or after the change, will have serious impact on the organisation.

The importance of IT as a change factor largely depends on the way in which IT was used before a change and how it is to be used after change.

Radical change affects both the relative importance of IT as a resource and the way in which the organisation manages it. This is illustrated by the case of Personal Care Ltd.

Example scenario

Personal Care Ltd

Personal Care is a manufacturing firm that produces toothpaste and shaving gel for a national market. Personal Care is traditionally organised: it has a sales and marketing department, two production plants, and a design and packaging department. Supporting these functional departments there is a financial and accounting department, a personnel department and an IT department. Personal Care is going through some rough patches. Arguments between sales representatives and packaging designers abound, plant managers complain about frequent adjustments of the production lines for shaving gel due to design changes. Profit margins on toothpaste are under pressure because of production inefficiencies. Finally, a rumour that persists throughout the organisation has it that the Board of Directors is considering selling the shaving gel activities to a big multinational.

The Board of Directors wants to restructure the organisation. It sees the need to change from the old, functional organisation structure to a product-oriented one. Its current aim is to have separate toothpaste and shaving gel divisions, each with their own sales, design, production, accounting and personnel departments, retaining only a few policy-making units in the central structure. The discussion among the Board members now focuses

---

on the IT department. Is it to be split up between the two product divisions and, if so, how?

One member of the Board argues for dividing the IT function in two. The arguments are that since both product divisions are to be responsible for their profit margins they must be able to control substantial overhead costs, such as those for IT; the financial administration system should be decentralised because the financial department will also be reorganised. Further, it has been hard to keep the sales information system up to date mainly because of the frequent changes in the shaving gel product line.

Decentralisation will provide the opportunity to change the functionality of the system in keeping with the different characteristics of the product lines; production scheduling was already separate for the two product lines; decentralisation merely formalises the previously existing product-oriented control.

Another member of the Board argues against dividing the IT department. The arguments are that all applications run on a single mainframe computer. Decentralisation implies that each division will want to have their 'own' system and that would increase cost; by keeping IT centralised the central structure can enforce its strategies on the two product divisions. Having two separate sales information systems means losing valuable information on the customers that buy both toothpaste and shaving gel, 60% of Personal Care's market.

It is only fair, runs the argument, that the central structure bears the operating cost of IT, since the Board itself profits most from the resulting management information and control.

The chairman of the Board is undecided. No easy compromise seems likely, since both distribution of power and the retention of some form of central control, while keeping costs down, are equally important issues. The main concern is that pursuing the desirable distribution of power while maintaining a central mainframe and common information systems will result in awkward arrangements at best.

Whatever the decision, the corporate strategy must recognise the impact of change on the use of IT and its impact in the business area.

2.5 IT and corporate strategy

If the way in which IT is managed is not changed, or if systems are not flexible enough, you will find that IT stands between you and the targeted results of change in corporate strategy. How important is IT in your organisation?

There are four broad categories for IT use:

- IT is used in **support** of the primary process of the organisation. IT is used for automating supporting processes, often of the administrative kind. This is the type of usage nearly all organisations have. It is typically not crucial for accomplishing the organisation's mission.

- IT is **part** of the primary process, carrying out part of the work that is considered core business (common in banks and other financial organisations). Fully automated production lines in industry are another example. IT used in this way has an impact on both short-term and long-term productivity. The flexibility of IT systems in this category influences the extent to which an organisation may be innovative in the market, e.g. develop new products, reach new customer groups.

- IT is a **management tool** for the organisation. The organisation's management uses IT to steer and control the organisation's processes. Blanket terms for this type of usage are Management Information System and Decision Support System.

- IT is used as a basis for **innovation and knowledge transfer**, as a tool to manage information that helps the organisation deal with external factors, i.e. the organisation's environment. Usually, this type of usage will remain fairly stable in times of change. If, however, knowledge is part of an organisation's core business, as in research institutes or high-tech environments, this type of usage affects the company's long-term innovative potential. It should then be classified in the second category.

Clearly, IT use within organisations often involves varying combinations of these four elementary categories.

2.6 Positioning IT in your organisation

When determining the position of IT, consider the role of managing the IT services and the criteria you may wish to employ to inform sourcing and service strategies (that is, IT Service Management – ITSM).

In thinking about the importance of IT and ITSM, you may want to consider the following:

- What proportion of the organisation's staff use IT to get their jobs done?
- Is there at least one part of the primary process that has been automated to such an extent that it would not, financially or organisationally, be possible to perform the process manually for a prolonged period of time?
- Do the customers of your organisation (or consumers of your products and services) use IT in order to obtain the organisation's products and services?
- Do customers or consumers use the organisation's IT directly or indirectly?
- Do staff blame 'the computer system' if something is wrong?
- Are management reports compiled using IT?
- What are the storage media in use?
- Are the organisation's products and services dependent on complex and intricate calculations or on recording, retrieving and analysing large volumes of data?

If IT is important now in your organisation, consider how important it will be after change takes place.

2.7 Options for dealing with IT

Corporate strategy should consider IT and ITSM in the context of the way in which IT is used and organised. In effect, what you are dealing with is the IT capability: the ability of the organisation to make best use of the benefits that IT can offer. Depending on the type of organisation you work in and the position of IT in your organisation, you will need to consider various options for dealing with IT, including:

- Option 1: prepare IT capability for an enabling and/or supporting role. In this situation, your strategy is of a timescale that allows such change.
- Option 2: change-as-you-go: change the IT capability in correspondence with the changes that occur in the business. This option requires a more intuitive approach than option 1. It entails making changes to IT as circumstances arise. It is the only option you have when you do not have enough time left to plan changes well in advance.
- Option 3: outsource. This option entails placing IT outside the scope of the changing organisation, at least as far as you are concerned. This option is only relevant if IT is neither part of the primary process nor supportive of the processes that are changing.

A corporate strategy should consider the future role of IT and ITSM. As mentioned earlier, although procurement of IT should be straightforward, its use is complicated by many factors. These include the following:

- IT capability does not equal IT department (an example is of a design aid that is used for product innovation and that is procured and managed by the Research and Development department).

- Non-routine IT tasks are closely connected to the skills and experience of individuals; these are very difficult to 'reorganise'.

- Certain IT components may fulfil a role in several or all four IT use categories. Think of an e-mail system that is used as a workflow management and production scheduling system as well. The complexity of such a system makes it hard to determine which aspects of it pose a problem in a change situation.

- Uncertainty: you really do not know what the future will bring, so demands on the organisation and on future IT position and usage are hard to determine.

Your decisions on certain aspects of IT may have painful consequences for others. For instance, when you decide to outsource your particular IT services, the corporate strategy should recognise the major impact on people in IT as well as technology and allow for proper management of difficult circumstances.

2.8 Preparing IT for radical change

Preparation requires posing questions such as the following.

- Which aspects of the corporate strategy will cause problems for business processes?

- Which aspects of the corporate strategy will cause problems for the way in which the business uses IT?

- What will be the position of IT in your organisation after the strategic changes and what effect will this have on IT functions and processes?

- Are there any distinguishable functions or processes in IT that are likely to differ following implementation of strategic changes? For example, will new information systems need to be developed or will existing systems be adapted?

- What external constraints should be taken into account (lack of funds, untrained staff, legally binding arrangements)?

You will find that, to gain insight into the effects of the change to the business and their consequences for IT, it is crucial to develop a view on how IT may serve to realise certain aspects of the change. Consider the following three roles of IT:

- The IT capability enables the change. IT is a driving force in the change process as the use of IT makes the change possible. This, for example, is the case when an organisation changes its process from mass production to Computer Integrated Manufacturing and is thus able to cater to new markets.

- The IT capability supports the change. Those activities that are important in controlling and effectuating the change are managed with the use of IT. An example is the automatic collection and reporting of financial data, which is used by the organisation's management to check profitability and set prices for its products.

- The IT capability reflects the change. Changes in the business must be reflected by corresponding changes in information systems, IT service provision and the IT infrastructure. For example, as a result of a legislative change a government department needs to adjust its procedures and forms. Part of the department's procedures had been automated and now the software needs to be adapted to comply with the changes in legislature.

Trying to determine the role of IT in the change process of course bears a resemblance to positioning IT in your organisation (Section 2.6). An important difference, however, is that at first you positioned IT by examining the actual situation, whereas now you are working from what is proposed in the corporate strategy. You are trying to predict the future. Bearing in mind the changes that are most likely to occur, you try to envisage a role for IT in the process.

2.8.1   Scenario-based planning

Run through possible scenarios and events that may result from the corporate strategy.

The events in particular scenarios are best generated through 'brainstorming'. It helps to have some kind of plot, such as 'best case', 'fierce competition', etc. Several scenarios emerge and then each scenario is elaborated upon by assessing the changes that the organisation must go through. Exploring and researching the changes necessary for the organisation's continued success is the crux of scenario-based planning.

To come to grips with the changes implied by a scenario, it is often helpful to think of changes in terms of quantitative and qualitative changes to:

- the organisation's administrative structure and processes
- the organisation's production process, methods and technology
- the organisation's products, services, reputation and image
- the organisation's labour force and culture.

There are a few additional 'rules of thumb':

- Use a 'team' approach, making a team responsible for each scenario, or use one team for all of them. The 'team' approach ensures that different views and perspectives are incorporated.

- Always adopt an even number of scenarios. Having an odd number means that the one in the middle will appear to be the most realistic scenario. Unfortunately realistic scenarios tend to blur issues.

- Have a 'sky's the limit' and a 'doom' scenario. The first lets you explore the boundaries of growth, the latter the limitations of the organisation.

Do not discard strange or seemingly far-fetched external events. When a strategic planning unit of a major company assumed the fall of the Berlin Wall in one scenario, they were laughed at by the Board. Several years later (and sooner than assumed) it became fact.

2.9 Planning for an uncertain future

The corporate strategy should enable IT to provide support (in the same way that IT should enable business).

Key to the success of the strategy (as with any major business or indeed IT or ITSM) programme is measurement of success. Define key performance indicators (KPIs) or critical success factors (CSFs) that you can – and do – measure. Your measurement framework will allow you to consider any further strategic (or perhaps operational) changes that you need to make to keep things on track.

2.10 Staying prepared

All preparation will be wasted if your corporate strategy is not maintained and of course refreshed according to change and the challenges ahead. That in itself is one of the goals of preparation: to become fit and to stay fit.

You now need to maintain a vigilant state. The vigilant state starts when it is decided that IT is part of the corporate strategy and it ends when change is implemented.

- **Scan the environment**. The responsibility for this activity can only lie with senior management. Collect and interpret information. Read newspapers, attend conferences, and talk with people in other organisations.

- **Assess IT capability**. Use outsiders and benchmarking for an objective viewpoint. Concentrate on the potential to function in a changing environment and the ability to enact specific, foreseeable changes.

- **Set preparation goals**. A planning group or committee should be involved here to gain commitment and drive. Use changes in perspective on the impending change as you go along. Ensure that realistic goals are set through knowledge gained from assessment of the IT capability.

- **Modify the current IT capability**. Involve current IT staff and management, with some 'new blood' or outsiders if 'people' is one of the problem areas. Make sure no new risks are introduced; allow experimentation without real changes. Change on the basis of existing software, skills, staff, organisation and procedures as much as possible.

- **Manage the current IT capability**. Maintain normal operations where possible. Fill any gaps that will remain useful. Think twice about major changes or upgrades.

2.11 Conclusion

The corporate strategy of any organisation is in effect an 'umbrella' for its overall objectives, providing a general strategic statement of intent from which the business and functional strategies can be developed.

Corporate strategists need to have a good understanding of the external environment of the business as a whole. This environment includes the interacting variables, issues, flows, forces, stakeholders and institutions bearing upon the effective strategic design, conduct and performance of the business – perhaps across international borders. Fundamental to the operation of most business today is IT; and fundamental to the way in which services are made available, irrespective of sourcing decisions or changes to delivery, is IT Service Management. If, as a business person you feel that decisions regarding IT need to be made but that you need help understanding positioning, importance, capability or use, involve your Chief Information Officer (CIO) and other senior ITSM personnel in the process.

3 IT GOVERNANCE

3.1 Key messages for the Board

IT governance is concerned with the cooperation between business and IT managers; this cooperation is required to achieve the business objectives that depend on IT capability. IT governance should be integrated with corporate governance. If your organisation already has a robust governance framework that incorporates IT, you should not separate out those aspects. ITIL is an important part of IT governance; CobiT and MIT are key considerations, but IT governance has a wider remit.

3.2 Introduction

It is generally accepted that IT is an integral part of the corporate drive for profitability and growth. It is also important for effective service delivery in not-for-profit organisations. However, the business return from IT expenditure is an ongoing concern and legislation now demands stricter controls on financial information, including controls covering provision and maintenance of IT systems.

The requirement for a better return on IT investments and the need to demonstrate control of IT risks are business concerns that need to be covered by an effective IT governance commitment.

This chapter explains the role of IT governance, its principles and processes. It draws on established best practice resources to clarify the underlying management philosophy and disciplines relating to IT governance. Understanding best practice IT governance will help your organisation improve the business benefits obtained from the exploitation of IT.

3.3 IT governance in context

- **Corporate strategy:** IT governance establishes the organisational capability for the implementation of corporate strategy by providing the framework for business/IT alignment and performance monitoring. With strategy providing the direction and pattern of corporate commitment, IT governance provides the organisational structure for delivering the IT components of this strategy.

- **Managing change:** IT governance identifies the key roles, authority and reporting arrangements for change programmes. IT governance provides the structure for continued organisational change that is enabled by IT.

- **Business and service continuity:** IT governance establishes the business priorities, responsibilities and controls required to ensure business continuity.

- **IT asset management:** IT governance provides the overarching framework for the exploitation of the organisation's IT assets.

- **Sourcing:** IT governance identifies the key business objectives and reporting arrangements that must be used to establish commercial sourcing agreements.

- **Knowledge management:** IT governance defines the management information required for effective governance, and the structure for IT-enabled knowledge management activities throughout the organisation.

3.4 What is IT governance?

3.4.1 Overview of governance

To establish a broad perspective on the role of IT governance it is useful to consider the role of governance generally.

The Institute on Governance (IOG) provides a helpful explanation of the role of governance. The IOG reminds us that the central purpose of governance is to provide a process through which a group of people make decisions that direct their collective efforts. The purpose of governance is summarised by the IOG as:

'Good governance is about both achieving desired results and achieving them in the right way.'

The *right way* is then qualified by explaining the organisational values that would be evident in best practice governance. These values include:

- participation – involvement of all stakeholders
- transparency – based on the free flow of information
- responsiveness – timely and relevant decisions
- equity – opportunities to be involved
- consensus oriented – decisions and actions supported by broad agreement
- effectiveness and efficiency – meeting needs with the best use of resources
- accountability – of decision-makers to stakeholders
- strategic vision – taking the long-term view.

Many of the ideas associated with governance can be seen to apply to IT governance, but to what extent do these values map on to the business challenge of exploiting IT capability?

3.4.2 A consensus view of IT governance

The most prominent resources for best practice IT governance are the MIT Sloan School of Management Center for Information Systems Research (MIT) and the IT Governance

Institute's Control Objectives for Information and related Technology (CobiT). These resources are consistent with one another and they are discussed in detail below. The general consensus is that IT governance contributes to business success by focusing on:

- *organisational structure*
  - management authority
  - decisions and influence
  - stakeholders and steering groups
- *business/IT management domains*
  - management disciplines and accountability
  - direction setting, expectations and results
- *performance monitoring*
  - goals and measures
  - learning.

Generally, the MIT resource has a stronger focus on organisational structures and accountability while the CobiT resource places more emphasis on management disciplines and risk control. Both highlight the need to be results orientated.

The consistent position given by this best practice work is that IT governance coordinates business/IT objectives, business/IT management commitments and associated performance measures. With this position it is important to consider what makes IT governance different from other management activity.

A simplified view of IT governance that brings together all the elements is given in Figure 3.1. The illustration highlights the fact that IT governance contributes to business success by ensuring that IT activity is continually in line with business requirements.

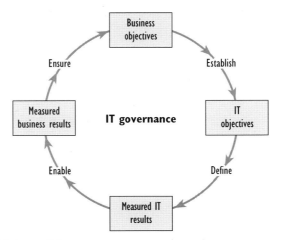

Figure 3.1 – Simplified view of IT governance

Figure used by permission of Reccan

3.5 Why is IT governance important?

Best practice IT governance recognises the need for a broad level of commitment across the organisation. A key role of IT governance is to ensure that any new or ongoing business IT solution is supported by both the business and IT management commitment. Because IT capability changes working methods it is also important to provide appropriate mechanisms for resolving problems associated with business dependencies and organisational change.

Equally important is the range of IT management disciplines and responsibilities that are required for the effective provision and maintenance of IT capability. A focus on IT management disciplines will help an organisation maintain a level of management commitment that is in line with the business priorities.

The MIT research into best practice IT governance concluded that IT governance is about 'leveraging the integrity of all the enterprise's people, not just the leaders'. For this to be achieved IT governance needs to be open and accessible. Therefore IT governance needs to involve all stakeholders, recognise that a range of business and IT management disciplines are involved and use business measures to monitor results.

Good IT governance recognises that IT offers a very wide range of business opportunities and business potential. The challenge is in selecting these IT opportunities and then ensuring that business and IT management commitment is fully secured.

Example case study for IT governance

A UK company with four very different business units maintained a central IT function that had attempted to optimise provision of its own responsibilities by standardising its IT methods.

The methodologies selected by the IT function were focused on large-scale IT projects but most of the business units needed rapid development solutions to maintain business agility. The difficulties developed into a bitter relationship between the IT function and the business units. IT projects were generally scrapped before the work was finished because delivery times were too long and the business conditions had changed.

A new IT director was appointed and responsibility for IT budgets was given back to the business units. A central IT governance group was set up as a link to the Board and each business unit maintained its own IT governance group. The IT function supported the business priorities for each IT governance group and influenced the use of common IT standards where this could be achieved.

As a result of this IT governance structure, business management became more actively involved in IT provision at both the business unit and company wide level.

Often business unit initiatives became the test environment for company wide infrastructure solutions. This approach reduced the cost, risk and development timescales. The overall impact was an increase in the business benefits obtained from IT exploitation, for the business units and the company as a whole.

3.6 Successful IT governance

Successful IT governance is concerned with realising business potential through the exploitation of IT. To briefly assess your organisation's IT governance effectiveness, consider the following questions.

- Do business and IT management openly and effectively cooperate to achieve the best result for the business?
- Is the energy and motivation of all staff positive towards the contribution of IT and the IT decisions process?
- Is the business expenditure on IT fully in line with the business objectives and priorities?
- Do IT initiatives generally meet or exceed business expectations?
- Do business management and staff fully exploit the current IT capability?
- Are business/IT controls in place to provide legally required assurance and business critical risk controls?

If you are not able to answer 'Yes' to all or most of these questions, then the integrity of your IT-based business solutions may be at risk, or your organisation could be wasting considerable resources through poor business/IT alignment.

3.7 Perspectives on IT governance

Within the opening paragraphs we provided a brief introduction to two prominent IT governance best practice resources to explain the broad scope of the IT governance agenda. To explore the benefits of these different, but complementary, resources we will review this best practice advice in more detail.

The work from MIT has looked at the nature of IT governance by investigating how business and IT managers in successful companies work together to exploit IT.

The IT Governance Institute, established in 1998 by the Information Systems Audit and Control Association (ISACA), was set up to sponsor research into effective IT governance. Some of its work is published as CobiT.

Many additional resources are available that provide information and advice on IT governance but some do not explicitly refer to the term *IT governance*. Most notably, topics such as *strategic IT management* and *IT Service Management* are significant aspects of the business/IT alignment challenge that are within the scope of IT governance.

Available IT governance guidelines either tend to focus on an *organisation and culture* view or take a *risk and control* perspective. Both interpretations are valid and integral to the role of IT governance; the perspective or emphasis required by an organisation will be influenced by which aspects of an organisation's management approach need attention. This will depend on the business and the business/IT management style that exists or is required. The management style is established by many factors but the business priorities and the organisation's tolerance for risk will have a very strong influence on the management approach used.

3.7.1 MIT perspective on IT governance

The interpretation of IT governance established by the MIT work provides an elegant and practical view of how senior business and senior IT managers in a large organisation see IT governance.

At this level of management, particularly in multi-business organisations, IT governance is seen as the working relationship between business and IT managers. MIT describes this working relationship as managing the harmonisation of what and how IT contributes to business success. This view of IT governance is illustrated in Figure 3.2.

This perspective is useful because it shows how the IT governance role depends on the business objectives and goals. Placing IT governance between business objectives and business performance goals helps to emphasise the position of IT and IT management as an enabler for achieving business success. The communication and coordination relationships (harmonising of the 'what' and 'how') draw out the point that different management perspectives covering culture, business process and IT capability need to work together for business success in exploiting IT.

3.7.2 IT governance styles, domains and mechanisms

The MIT work investigated the patterns of input and decision-making associated with IT to identify how the decision domains, structure of responsibility, and IT governance processes worked within over 250 mixed business organisations. This is illustrated in Figure 3.3.

The list of *IT governance styles* identified shows the diverse business structures that need to be recognised by IT governance. The terms *anarchy* and *feudal* make the point that

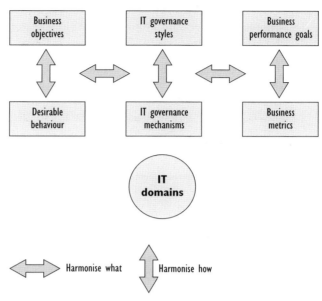

Figure 3.2 – Interpreting the MIT IT governance view

IT governance styles	IT domains	IT governance mechanisms
• Business monarchy • IT monarchy • Feudal • Federal • Anarchy	• Principles • IT infrastructure • IT architecture • Business applications • IT investment	• Executive committee • IT councils • Architecture committee • Capital and budget approval • Service level agreements • Chargeback • Process teams with IT membership

Figure 3.3 – Interpreting the MIT view of IT governance structures

some organisations may have good business reasons for not progressing coordinated IT decisions. In this situation IT information sharing would probably be a better IT governance policy than IT standardisation.

IT (decision) domains identify the areas where IT decisions are made and the *IT governance mechanisms* characterise the IT governance processes being used to help make or enforce the IT decisions.

The MIT work has shown that organisations successful with IT governance often had different IT governance styles for each IT decision domain. An example of this might be a 'federal' approach to IT infrastructure but a 'business monarchy' (central control) approach for IT investment decisions.

IT governance was found to be most effective when decisions were clearly linked to the main business performance metric such as Return on Assets (ROA), Revenue, Revenue/Employee or Market Capitalisation.

The MIT best practice research concluded that IT governance is concerned with 'specifying the decision rights and accountability framework to encourage desirable behaviour in the use of IT'. The research also concluded that effective IT governance used the ingenuity of all the organisation's people in a way that retained the commitment to its overall vision and principles.

3.7.3 CobiT perspective on IT governance

The IT Governance Institute's CobiT work offers a different perspective on IT governance. It provides a business level view of a broader range of IT management disciplines that need to be covered to achieve effective IT governance.

The scope of the CobiT IT governance disciplines is defined by the domain and process areas shown in Figure 3.4. The CobiT view of IT governance defines a lifecycle of IT management activities that contribute to the successful provision of IT capability. CobiT also emphasises the importance of performance monitoring that helps to assess business impact, measure IT process efficiency and control IT-related risk.

Planning and organisation		Delivery and support	
PO1	Define a strategic IT plan	DS1	Define and manage service levels
PO2	Define the information architecture	DS2	Manage third-party services
PO3	Determine technology direction	DS3	Manage performance and capacity
PO4	Define the IT organisation and relationships	DS4	Ensure continuous service
PO5	Manage the IT investment	DS5	Ensure system security
PO6	Communicate management aims and direction	DS6	Identify and allocate costs
PO7	Manage human resources	DS7	Educate and train users
PO8	Ensure compliance with external requirements	DS8	Assist and advise customers
PO9	Assess risks	DS9	Manage the configuration
PO10	Manage projects	DS10	Manage problems and incidents
PO11	Manage quality	DS11	Manage data
		DS12	Manage facilities
		DS13	Manage operations
Acquisition and implementation		**Monitoring**	
AI1	Identify automated solutions	M1	Monitor the processes
AI2	Acquire and maintain application software	M2	Assess internal control adequacy
AI3	Acquire and maintain technology infrastructure	M3	Obtain independent assurance
AI4	Develop and maintain procedures	M4	Provide for independent audits
AI5	Install and accredit systems		
AI6	Manage change		

Figure 3.4 – CobiT IT governance domains and process areas

The list of CobiT IT governance domains is very comprehensive. It would be difficult to argue that any of the 34 management disciplines is not relevant to the successful business exploitation of IT.

CobiT's business level interpretation of these IT management disciplines helps to explain the importance of the IT governance agenda. CobiT is a framework and resource that should be used to identify what IT management commitment is required rather than how this commitment is achieved. CobiT relies on other industry guidelines such as ITIL, the ISO 9000 family of standards, including ISO 9001 and ISO/IEC 90003 and ISO/IEC 27001 to provide the detailed guidelines required to implement these IT management processes.

3.7.4   CobiT IT governance structure

Within CobiT all the IT management processes are defined using a common structure that positions the business value of the IT management discipline and then outlines the key tasks that deliver this discipline. Measurement is covered by focusing on the process objectives and the measures required for process efficiency. CobiT defines IT governance as the framework for defining the desired results that are needed to direct and monitor the provision of IT capability. The structure used by CobiT to define the IT governance process areas is shown in Figure 3.5.

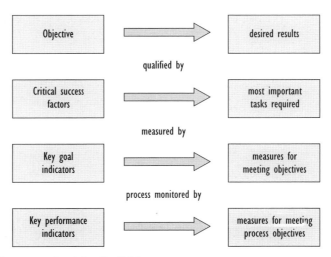

Figure 3.5 – Structure used to define CobiT 4.0 process areas

For each IT management process, a maturity model is defined that can be used to assess the current status and establish what maturity level is appropriate for the business.

CobiT, and other resources from the IT Governance Institute (see Appendix C), provide a very rich source of IT management wisdom. The strength of CobiT is in the range of IT management topics covered and in the detailed definition of what needs to be covered by each process area. CobiT is an important risk and control resource for IT assurance and a powerful resource for developing the processes that are required to support an effective commitment to IT governance.

3.8 The IT governance challenge

IT governance is important because IT capability can have a far-reaching impact on the organisation. In a dynamic corporate environment there are many conflicting priorities that can make it difficult to establish commitment to the IT priorities. The situation is harder for multi-business organisations that have a more diverse range of business activities.

Some of the problems include:

- business and IT managers with different views on what is best for the organisation
- requirements that cut across organisational structures and management styles – because of authority, accountability and management boundaries
- different views on current versus future value to the organisation
- conflicting objectives – what gets rewarded gets done!
- overall complexity and dynamics within the organisation
- limited investment budgets
- internal politics.

The problem is that the division of responsibilities and management structure, essential for a large organisation to be successful, could become an inhibiting factor when common interests need to be identified and resolved. IT governance is concerned with resolving the decisions and commitments associated with IT exploitation that is in the common interest.

3.9 The organisational challenge

Business and IT managers can all have different views on the value of IT. It is healthy for an organisation to have management expertise focused on different business and IT management activity because specialisation and focus help to optimise business productivity. However, this focus can inhibit the organisation's ability to stay agile and fully exploit IT because IT introduces organisational change.

Business and IT management must clearly remain focused on their own area of business operations but also need to be involved with wider business concerns and decisions that might disrupt or change their own area of responsibility.

Uncoordinated IT commitment will result in higher costs and damage to staff productivity; it could also inhibit the development of integrated business processes. Because of this, and because IT is such a pervasive aspect of most organisations, it is essential that business and IT management cooperate to ensure the success of any IT initiatives. This can be seen in Figure 3.6.

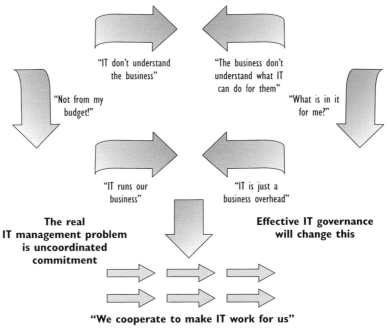

Figure 3.6 – Business and IT management cooperation

Figure used by permission of Reccan

Within IT governance the organisational challenge is to ensure that business priorities drive IT commitments. To achieve this, all those involved must understand and actively assist in the integration of new working methods facilitated by IT.

3.10   Maintaining a successful IT governance commitment

3.10.1   Organisational structures

To implement or maintain a successful IT governance commitment it is important that stakeholder representation is coordinated up to, and including, Board level responsibilities. The structure of this coordination will generally follow the existing organisational structure of the business (for example, centralised or federal) and the corresponding management style within the company as a whole. Business level forums supported by IT management representation need to take the main decision-making roles but, when appropriate, technical forums will need to be established to provide specialist decision support. The MIT resource covers this topic in depth and has detailed advice on maintaining an appropriate IT governance structure.

Management authority and responsibility should ensure that the focus on business objectives and priorities is maintained within the IT governance structure. The real challenge for the IT governance groups will be to encourage and support the innovative environment required to continually challenge the business opportunities and risk associated with IT exploitation. In many ways the IT governance agenda can be seen as a portfolio management responsibility where the work priority is to maximise the use of business resources and balance the commitment to current and future business objectives.

3.10.2   Performance monitoring

An important component of IT governance is the requirement to monitor the contribution that IT makes to the overall business objectives. The Kaplan and Norton Balanced Scorecard approach, an accepted governance level performance management tool, can and should be used at the IT management level. CobiT is an excellent resource for developing IT performance monitoring but care needs to be taken to use all four Balanced Scorecard categories (covering financial, customer, process and learning perspectives) to achieve meaningful performance objectives and monitoring.

Performance monitoring will be used by different groups within the organisation. For example, Board level managers will be interested in how IT contributes to the overall business objectives not in the IT performance statistics. For all stakeholders, the basic principle of Balanced Scorecard is 'measurement motivates'. For this benefit to be realised the IT governance coordination must ensure that all stakeholders understand and are committed to the performance objectives being used.

3.10.3   A process for coordinating change

A very useful explanation of the IT governance challenge is provided by a discipline called *systems thinking*. In his book, *The Fifth Discipline*, Peter Senge describes systems thinking as the discipline for seeing wholes. A systems-thinking approach promotes a shift of mind from linear cause and effect and snapshots to seeing interrelationships and a process of change. This mindset shift is exactly what IT governance needs to promote and use.

In practical terms IT governance must be set up to recognise the interrelationships between management domains within the business and within IT. Because IT has such a pervasive role, recognition that IT governance is facilitating change ensures that all those involved or affected by change will be able to accommodate the changes required.

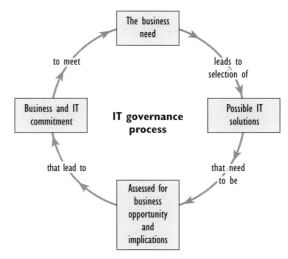

Figure 3.7 – IT governance – a process for coordinating change

Figure used by permission of Reccan

Using a systems-thinking perspective IT governance can be described as a process for coordinating change, as shown in Figure 3.7. The principles of IT governance can then be explained by the following stages:

1   You have a problem that involves a significant number of stakeholders (such as an organisation seeking to improve revenue through IT investment).

2   The best approach to solving this problem is to look at the range of solutions available for this problem area. However, you should recognise that a solution that worked for others may not be right for your situation (make sure you understand the real problem that this IT solution has solved before).

3   Given the proviso in stage 2, it may be advantageous to examine the solution to understand how it can change your situation and where some compromise might be required (an IT governance process to examine the opportunity and implications).

4   If the solution appears to be a good fit, with some compromise, then the actions to improve your situation can be taken with a higher level of confidence (business and IT management make the commitment).

This approach to IT exploitation is in principle never-ending; it is best conducted with all interested parties but ensure that they understand the process so that they will understand the consequences and fully commit to the actions agreed (this is the IT governance remit).

With this coordinating-change view it can be seen how the activities associated with IT governance are guided by the corporate management agenda where the business priorities are established as 'the business need'. The role of IT governance is to use these business priorities to direct and guide the organisational changes associated with IT exploitation.

Because cooperation from multiple stakeholders is required the values associated with governance will generally apply to IT governance.

The coordinating-change view shows that the most important aspect of IT governance is to maintain a productive process that will ensure IT commitments are aligned with business priorities. To achieve this alignment it is essential that all interested parties are involved to ensure they make the commitment to the actions required and accept any compromise that needs to be made.

3.10.4   The essence of IT governance

The two best practice resources we have identified (MIT and CobiT) can be seen as 'possible IT solutions' within the IT governance process outlined above (Figure 3.7). The MIT resource can be used to improve the effectiveness of the organisational structure and the IT decision groups, whereas CobiT can be used to improve the effectiveness of a broad range of IT governance processes and provide IT risk assurance.

Although all the best practice IT governance resources identified are helpful for refining your organisation's IT governance effectiveness, the majority of 'possible IT solutions' will be developed by looking at business objectives and recognising how IT can successfully contribute. 'Possible IT solutions' will cover any response to business needs that has an IT implication. In all situations, the essence of IT governance is the ongoing and coordinated commitment that makes 'possible IT solutions' successful business solutions.

4 MANAGING CHANGE

4.1 Key messages for the Board

Change affects all aspects of the business. It may be a strategic response to changes in the business environment, which will be led and directed by the Management Board. Or it may be a minor operational change, refining existing products or services. Whatever the change, its impact needs to be understood and managed.

4.2 Chapter summary

This chapter examines the challenges of managing change, and the key issues that the Board and senior management must deal with in a change initiative. It outlines best practices, such as ITIL, and provides concepts and questions to guide senior management in their decision-making. It reminds senior management of the close relationship between the business and IT, and the consequences that poorly managed IT can have on the business. Finally, it examines managing change from an organisational perspective revealing that people are the most important elements in managing change.

Recent changes to legislation enforce accountability on senior management and require a heightened awareness to what is going on in the business. It is no longer acceptable to say, 'I didn't know'. Ignorance is no excuse for breaking the law. With regards to IT, this means knowing, directing and monitoring IT – through the Chief Information Officer (CIO) and senior IT managers who sit on the Board and in senior management positions of the business.

In order to achieve this, the Board and senior management must direct and take a hands-on, holistic view to managing change; this must include working with people, processes and technology.

4.3 What is change?

Change is 'doing things differently', whether a radical transformation or a minor alteration to current procedures – or anything between these two extremes that is different from before.

As external environmental factors become increasingly complex, businesses today must lead, follow or get left behind – a simple statement to make perhaps, but not an easy one to follow.

We know that globalisation increases both the competition and the complexity of business interaction. In order to survive, businesses have to be in more parts of the world, manage a diversity of relationships, and get products and services to market better and faster than the competition. In doing so, businesses also have to recognise and comply with national and global legislation, understand the impact of the economy on the business and leverage technology accordingly. Heightened security measures only add to the complexities. Even businesses, public and private, that are not global have to be aware of how these external factors affect their business.

As IT continues to take a more central role in business strategy and operations, senior management and Boards must understand the interface and relationships with IT operations. IT is not an add-on, or a 'nice to have'; it is a business-critical area that must be well understood, analysed and questioned. In order to do this effectively, IT must understand the business, and the business must understand IT. There must be CIO and IT representation at Board, executive and senior management levels to ensure business alignment.

Change can be driven by external forces such as privacy laws and the Sarbanes-Oxley legislation, or it can be driven by internal forces looking to increase profitability, growth, staff, customer retention or market penetration. Internal forces result in changes to internal processes, people, technology, organisational structure, span of control, etc. These changes are almost always tied in with or are the catalyst for changes to the IT infrastructure.

4.4 Why is it important to manage change?

All change needs to be managed.

John P. Kotter of the Harvard Business School tells us that it is important to manage change. Without the required Change Management practices and procedures to move it forward and embed it into an organisation, most change initiatives fail.

Not only do most fail, but most also ignore the key ingredient to successful Change Management – people.

Research shows that when change is introduced:

- 10% of employees will be supportive
- 60% of employees will be ambivalent
- 30% of employees will be actively opposed.

Research also shows that people go through stages during a change that often involve:

- saying goodbye to old ways that made them successful and were part of their work identities

- shifting into neutral, coping with uncertainties, and coming to grips with new ways

- moving forward and behaving in the new ways.

The Harvard Business School identifies four stages in the reaction to change:

- shock

- defensive retreat

- acknowledgement

- acceptance and adaptation.

These examples show that change must be managed – or serious consequences may befall the organisation.

4.5 Top five questions that the business should ask to be assured that change is being managed effectively

To be assured that change is being managed effectively, the business must work with three key aspects of the organisation – people, process and technology. Gaps in any of these areas should be uncovered and dealt with accordingly. Gaps within people management especially, should be closed, as people often resist or even sabotage change.

Five key questions should be considered before moving forward.

- Has the need for change, its costs and benefits, and the impact and risks of the change to the business been carefully researched, analysed and approved? Who has approved the change?

- Have consequences been researched? What are they, what are the risks, what are the cost/benefit ratios?

- Have plans been made for dealing with instability? What are the plans, who is going to deal with this? At what point do we have a serious problem?

- Does the change plan thoroughly cover all aspects of the lifecycle of the change, including Configuration, Change and Release Management?

- Have all aspects of people, process and technology been considered and planned for in the change? Accountabilities: who is accountable and for what?

These questions are intended to prompt you to:

- involve IT in the planning

- ensure continuity of service during transition

- ensure robust fall-back plans

- ensure accountabilities for fall-back plans

- plan and approve testing
- define what is to be done, by whom and by when
- allocate responsibility and ownership for business and IT systems
- plan for and deal with legacy issues appropriately.

Assessing whether change should happen

- Make sure you want to change and that it is really necessary
- What is the change driver? Why? For whom?
- What is the scope of the change? What parts of the business will be affected?
- What new or altered business competencies are required?
- What changes in IT deployment are required?
- Can we use existing IT capabilities? If so, which ones?
- Can the business and the IT service provider take the business from where it is now to where we want it to be?
- How long will it take?
- How much will it cost?
- Are all requirements needed?
- Are all deadlines firm?

4.6 The evidence the Board needs to demonstrate that issues are being addressed appropriately

As the Board is accountable to shareholders, it must continuously monitor and look for evidence that issues are being addressed appropriately. The following provides a checklist and roadmap to help.

The Board and senior management must request this evidence:

- An organisational analysis that assesses the people and culture of the organisation and their readiness for change. This type of analysis puts change into the context of sponsorship, leadership, motivation, measurements, customer focus, rewards, prior experience with change, and organisational hierarchy to measure acceptance or resistance to change. It can be used as one indicator of how likely the change is to be adopted.

- An approved business plan and presentation that shows direct tie-in with corporate objectives, current departmental and programme planning, and the credentials and signature of the approver.

- Effective IT governance to ensure that IT projects are aligned with corporate objectives and that the IT expenditure is appropriate for the business requirements.

- Demonstrated knowledge, skill and ability in IT Service Management best practices, including, but not exclusive to, ITIL best practices, especially in the Configuration, Change and Release Management processes; ISO/IEC 20000; and total quality management practices.

- Demonstrated knowledge, skill, ability and certification in programme and project management.

- Comprehensive programme plan outlining roles, responsibilities and activities for managing people, processes and technology, throughout the lifecycle of the change.

- Human Resources planning document and evidence of alignment with the organisation's Human Resources policies and procedures, including, but not limited to, organisational culture, hiring practices, recognition and reward, training and development, compensation, job descriptions, leadership styles and financial controls.

- Business continuity, risk management planning document to ensure that changes within the IT infrastructure do not have a negative impact on the business. This should clearly outline both risk management and security management issues.

- Due diligence report – showing compliance with regulations and guidelines.

A word of caution is needed here. Collecting this information is a lot of work that many will argue there is not time or need for. Their argument, driven perhaps by funding or competition, is fair – business has to keep moving and growing. However, these activities are imperative to the success of the change initiative. Without thorough research and analysis, the change effort will fail.

The business needs to know and understand the IT infrastructure – not knowing only creates confusion and indecision. The following list should be used for examining the strengths and weaknesses of the IT infrastructure. Each area should be viewed from various angles and from various roles within the organisation.

4.6.1 To determine the size of the IT infrastructure

- Financial budget – the percentage of annual budgets spent on the IT infrastructure

- Number of staff – number of full time equivalents (FTEs)

- Installed base – the number of workstations in the enterprise compared with other office items such as furniture and administrative forms. Indication of the effect of IT on staff's working patterns

■ Authority level – the level at which decisions are made in the IT organisation compared to the level at which they are made enterprise-wide

■ Legacy issues – what are they?

4.6.2 To determine the complexity of the IT infrastructure

■ The nature and degree of dependencies – determining the level of dependency in the IT infrastructure.

4.6.3 To determine the stakeholders within the IT infrastructure

■ Who they are – determine who they are and the amount of influence that can be exerted on IT. For example, if IT is partially outsourced, you may have little control.

4.6.4 To determine the achievement of the IT infrastructure

■ Value-added – determine the value that IT adds to the business. Include business added value, quality, capacity, cost IT, control IT and change IT capabilities

■ In addition to assessing the IT infrastructure, it is useful to assess the level of organisational maturity including the financial/economic state as well as the technological state of the organisation.

Example of a change effort that resulted in a business loss

In 2001, a large grocery store chain completed its migration to a new point-of-sale inventory and cash register system. The rollout was well planned, the implementation was well managed, and the project ended successfully. People, process and technology were aligned and the system was up and running. In 2004, an upgrade was made to the system. The upgrade, seemingly a small project compared to the main change earlier, was not managed as carefully. Service outages started to crop up; cash registers did not work; inventory numbers were not accurate. On a particular Sunday, 10% of the stores open 24-7 had their system go down for an eight-hour period. Customers were asked to put down their goods and leave, and customers trying to enter the store found the doors locked. The loss of business was substantial and could be measured – loss of revenue, loss of customers and loss of potentially new customers. What could not be measured was the impact on families who might, in the middle of the night, have had a sick child or parent requiring cold or pain medication. Year-end results, however, showed a drop in revenue for stores open 24-7.

In this example, the impact of change was so much greater than first

---

realised. Planning upfront, adherence to best practices and controls could have resulted in positive rather than negative year-end figures. A poorly managed IT change in this example had a major impact on the business.

4.7 Managing change from the top down

The Board and senior management of organisations are responsible for organisational strategy and goals, and must ensure that change initiatives are aligned with the business and adequately connected and controlled throughout the organisation. OGC's *Managing Successful Programmes* (MSP) is a best practice approach for managing change.

The Board and senior management must take time to ensure that managers involved know how to manage change effectively, and if not, provide training and coaching to reinforce the desired behaviours. For example, managers must know that communication is key – communications with staff should be conducted openly and honestly. Managers must also know that resistance has to be sought out, listened to and responded to appropriately.

The Board must ensure that there is management and control of a change, together with a structured approach to programme and project management.

OGC's *Successful Delivery Toolkit*, a single point of reference on the OGC website, describes proven good practice for procurement, programmes, projects, risk and Service Management. It provides critical questions about capability and project delivery and gives practical advice on how to improve.

The OGC website can be found at www.ogc.gov.uk and should be used for reference and guidance.

Briefly, portfolio management, programme management and project management must be integrated to align the processes and people involved in change initiatives. The closer they are aligned, the higher the probability that the change effort will be moved forward successfully.

Portfolio management should manage programmes, which in turn should oversee project management. Alignment should always be strong. A project that does not fit with the overall portfolio management is useless to the organisation and should be stopped.

4.8   ITIL best practices – optimising Change, Configuration and Release Management

Controlling changes to the IT infrastructure and services across distributed systems, multiple locations and support groups can be a daunting experience and requires careful planning and management. IT infrastructures must have mature processes and accountability, and follow strict standards and best practices in order to obtain and maintain optimisation. The ITIL framework provides such best practices and when used effectively can manage and control changing environments. For the purposes of this chapter, the Change, Configuration and Release Management processes will be discussed in terms of how they can be used in managing change effectively. Details on the processes can be found in OGC's ITIL *Service Support* and *Service Delivery* books.

The three processes – Change, Configuration and Release Management – should be well understood by the IT organisation and embedded into its policies and procedures. To be most effective, a central function should be responsible for their planning and implementation. The Service Level Management process should also be included. Figure 4.1 illustrates the relationship between the processes.

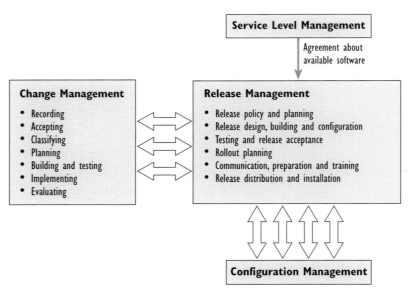

Figure 4.1 – Relationship between ITIL processes

These ITIL processes, Change, Configuration and Release Management, optimise the management of change. Whether changes are made to the IT infrastructure because of problems, or because of improvements or cost savings, change-related incidents are likely to occur. These incidents are likely to affect the products or services that the organisation provides. The severity of the impact may result in downtime, which depending on the nature of the business can result in loss of revenue or service. This again affects the business and should be of great interest to the Board and senior management.

4.8.1 The Change Management process

ITIL provides guidance on the Change Management process and should be followed whenever changes are made to hardware, software, documentation and procedures associated with the training, support and maintenance of live systems. Employees involved in any part of this should know ITIL well, and be appropriately qualified. See Appendix B for more information.

The goal of the Change Management process is to ensure that standardised methods and procedures are used for the handling of all changes, in order to minimise the impact of change-related incidents to the business. ITIL provides information on how to set up a Change Management process that includes procedures, tools, and dependencies that are necessary to plan for, implement and run Change Management.

The Change Management process approves or denies proposed changes through the Change Advisory Board (CAB). The CAB is made up of people from other functions within the organisation, ensuring organisation-wide involvement. A well-rounded Change Management process should have the following attributes:

- inputs
  - RFCs – Requests for Change
  - CMDB – Configuration Management Database (to document assets and their relationships)
  - FSC – Forward Schedule of Changes
- activities of Change Management
  - filtering changes
  - managing changes and the change process
  - chairing the CAB (and emergency committee)
  - reviewing and closing RFCs
  - management reporting
- outputs
  - FSC
  - RFCs
  - CAB minutes and actions
  - Change Management reports.

Managing change effectively is about planning, controlling, managing risk, minimising disruption, communicating, implementing and measuring. The Change Management process manages changes to the operations at day-to-day level.

As a best practice, the CAB should work closely with programme and project management teams to ensure that change issues and impacts are cascaded throughout the organisation. Project management standards from PRINCE2 or the Project Management Institute (PMI) should be followed.

The Board may want to periodically audit for compliance and check the following:

- randomly selected RFCs – normal, urgent and standard changes to audit that they are correctly logged, assessed and actioned
- change records – to determine if change reviews are carried out on time
- Forward Schedule of Changes – to check whether adhered to
- CAB meeting action items – to check if they are followed up and resolved
- documentation – to determine if it is accurate, current and complete.

4.8.2   The Configuration Management process

To be effective and efficient, businesses need to control their IT infrastructure and services. Configuration Management provides a model of the infrastructure or service by identifying, controlling, maintaining and verifying the versions of Configuration Items (CIs) in existence.

CIs include services, servers, environments, equipment, desktops, applications, licences and facilities. These CIs are recorded and managed in the Configuration Management Database (CMDB). The CMDB records this information and the changes to it, as well as identifying the 'owners' of the item and the relationships between the items, providing transparent and accessible information.

A good Configuration Management process will have the following:

- a robust Configuration Management Database that shows the relationships
- software and document libraries
- Definitive Software Library
- Definitive Hardware Library
- licence management controls and standards.

Review and audits should be done regularly to ensure that:

- staff are trained to perform the Configuration Management activities effectively
- Configuration Management activities are audited against Configuration Management plans
- the selection of CIs is appropriate to support and control Problem, Change and Release Management
- IT Service Management staff have access to current, accurate and complete configuration records and data.

Before a major release or change, an audit of a specific CI may be necessary. An audit should provide a clear picture of the current situation and identify discrepancies between the CMDB and the customer's environment. These audits also check that change and release records have been authorised during the Change Management process.

Management reporting should cover:

- the results of configuration audits
- information on any non-registered or inaccurately registered CIs detected and their corrective action
- growth and capacity information
- the value and location of CIs.

There should be strong ties between Configuration Management and the finance and purchasing functions within the organisation. Configuration Management is responsible for making the finance function aware of changes in the location and condition of all property classified as a CI.

4.8.3 The Release Management process

The Release Management process should be well in place and work closely with any changes, taking a holistic view of a change to an IT service – to ensure the successful rollout of software and related hardware.

The focus of Release Management is to protect the live environment and ensure that the checks and balances are in place. It deploys formal checks and procedures. As Release Management becomes more efficient, releases are better managed and planned, training is better orchestrated and documentation is of a higher quality. As a result end-users are less disrupted and more productive.

Management should ensure that:

- the Release Management process is in place
- staff understand the scope of this process
- a concise Release Policy is written and used, and includes:
  - release naming and numbering conventions
  - definition of major and minor releases
  - a policy of issuing emergency fixes
  - identification of business-critical times to avoid for implementation
  - the policy on the production and degree of testing of back-out plans
  - a description of the Release Management control process
- hardware release and distribution procedures
- software release and distribution procedures.

Key performance indicators (KPIs) for Release Management are:

- releases built, implemented on time and within budget
- accuracy of the Definitive Software Library
- legal compliance with all software and licensing
- a post implementation review carried out on all release activities.

Management should know the number of minor and major releases during a given reporting period and problems caused in the live environment.

4.9 Critical success factors for managing change

To increase the success rate of business transformation, the following must occur:

- strong vision, support and leadership from the top
- clarity of strategic objectives and the benefits to be realised *before* the investment of resources is made
- a strong imperative to change (burning platforms)
- a clear vision that is communicated to everyone affected
- governance that is separated from delivery of the change
- ongoing and consistent communication of benefits and the status of current progress
- expectations that are managed.

John P. Kotter of the Harvard Business School has spent over a decade observing and researching organisational transitions and change. His research indicates that there are at least eight common mistakes that organisations make:

- allowing too much complacency
- failing to create a sufficiently powerful guiding coalition
- underestimating the power of vision
- under-communicating the vision
- permitting obstacles to block the vision
- failing to create short-term wins
- declaring victory too soon
- neglecting to anchor changes firmly in the corporate culture.

In response to this, Kotter designed an eight-stage model for implementing change. Each stage is associated with one of the eight fundamental errors that undermine transformation efforts as listed above. The first four steps help to 'defrost' a hardened status quo. They are:

■ establishing a sense of urgency

■ creating the guiding coalition

■ developing a vision and strategy

■ communicating the change vision.

The next stages then introduce new practices:

■ empowering a broad base of people to take action

■ generating short-term wins

■ consolidating gains and producing even more change.

The final stage is required to ground the changes in the corporate culture, and make them stick:

■ anchoring new approaches into the culture.

Kotter asserts that all of the stages must be worked through in order, and completely, to achieve successful change. Skipping even a single step creates problems. People under pressure to show results will often skip the warm-up or defrosting activities, thereby barely establishing a solid enough base on which to proceed. Failing to reinforce earlier stages results in the sense of urgency dissipating, or the guiding coalition breaking up. Without the follow-through, which takes place in the final step, the finish line will not be reached and the changes will not stick.

5 BUSINESS AND SERVICE CONTINUITY

5.1 Key messages for the Board

Business continuity should take account of the extended enterprise, not just the immediate organisation. It is important to consider collaborative arrangements outside the organisation. Reputational/brand risks must be planned for just as much as loss of revenue.

5.2 Executive summary

Business continuity is about the provision of an operating framework that helps the business develop its products and services and at the same time prevent or limit disruption, interruption or loss by ensuring efficient recovery to acceptable or normal levels of operating capacity. This chapter focuses on IT service continuity, which covers the IT elements of the overall business continuity plan.

However, IT service continuity can be seen as cost rather than insurance, and no longer does IT service continuity just mean 'disaster recovery'. It is more relevant to understand the importance of IT to the business.

This chapter looks at the demands that businesses in today's modern economy have for continuous IT service provision. This must be done in an environment where the demand for flexibility and speed in IT service has to be balanced with the increasing needs for availability and security.

> **Case study**
>
> In late 2000, a UK-based insurance company planned for a significant upgrade of their data storage capability. In early 2001 that storage capability failed for technical reasons and the company did not have adequate disaster recovery arrangements in place.
>
> This failing was caused by a combination of people, process and technology; through a lack of validation and operational acceptance; insufficient risk management; and unproven recovery procedures.
>
> In late 2001, that organisation ceased to trade.

Specifically, this chapter explains why someone in the IT organisation must be given the mission to protect the production environment, using operational risk management and IT governance principles to ensure that everything is done to prevent the implementation of risk and defect. At the same time the IT organisation needs to know what to do if the 'doomsday scenario' actually happens.

Research indicates that where a large organisation currently has poor continuity planning and processing, then it could take up to five years to implement fully effective continuity planning.

The cycle of 'prevent, detect, correct' has been around for a long time, but never before has this been so crucial. Previously we were concerned with single/internal IT systems when downtime meant some parts of the business could not operate. We are now dealing with customer-facing, business-critical services, where even a short period of downtime can mean the end of your business.

5.3   IT service continuity in context

The requirements for IT service continuity sit alongside those in the other chapters of this book.

How the organisation is structured and governed; how we manage change within our business and operating models; how the organisation ensures it utilises the assets and knowledge of the business; all of these have aspects of risk and a need for control.

Business continuity demands that within the IT operations we assess and manage the risks of all changes (whether these are people, process or technology), that we operate legally and morally, with sufficient governance and control to ensure we meet the aims of the business. Services and processes should be ranked according to their contribution to the business goals, usually criticality to customer and client service, then essential support services and finally the discretionary services that do not directly contribute to the goals.

The increasing demands for IT governance place a greater accountability on the Board to ensure that financial information is appropriately protected and maintained. Senior management must communicate the imperative of risk and express this in ways that explain the business, personal and social benefits. At the same time we must ensure that expenditure on IT resources and assets is justified.

The continued increase in demand for IT personnel with more skills, deeper knowledge and wider experience means that organisations must find ways of retaining and exploiting knowledge within the enterprise. Losing key personnel with key knowledge can be as devastating as losing a key application or database, so do organisations have adequate succession planning in place?

Where key processing and services have been globally sourced or locally outsourced, organisations must ensure that these providers have effective continuity processes and plans, that these are tested regularly and that they underpin the organisation's own continuity needs.

5.4   What is IT service continuity?

Organisations must be vigilant and well prepared and make arrangements to deal with the impact of a major incident or disaster on their business. This means that you need to understand the essential assets, infrastructure, services, processes, people and facilities that provide and support your mission-critical business services.

IT service continuity is the term used to define the strategies and plans in place to assure this provision of service and ensure that this is in support of the overall business continuity process.

Regulatory and legislative requirements mean that organisations must be able to demonstrate that they have the necessary arrangements in place to adequately respond to major incidents and disasters.

In order to understand the importance of these components, it is sensible to take some core business transactions and try to map these transactions across the components, providing an end-to-end transaction map. This will also enable the IT service provider to understand the impact of the service on the business. These maps will also provide operational and service architectures that are complementary – the organisational and technical architectures that most businesses have.

To test your organisation's continuous service capability, ask yourself the following questions.

- Do you know what your mission-critical business services are? How do you decide?
  - Organisations should consider the impact of their business products and services on their customers, shareholders and principal stakeholders. You should also give consideration to expectations of quality and timescales for the provision of these products and services.
- Do you regularly assess the threats to those mission-critical business services?
- Do you have strategies in place to prevent and detect those threats?
- Are there plans in place to repair, recover and restore service and operations?
- Is there regular and scheduled testing of those plans to ensure the plans are appropriate?

- Are the plans maintained and kept aligned with changes to business and IT demands?

- Are arrangements in place to ensure the security of the data, facilities and personnel involved in the provision of your services?

- Do you have acceptance criteria to ensure that projects and changes to services consider continuity and do not have a detrimental impact on other services?

- Do you have processes and measures to manage the recovery and restoration of services if a major incident occurs (or any incident that affects the availability and reliability of services)?

- Do your managed service and outsource providers have tested procedures in place that meet your requirements? Have you tested this?

- Are you aware of the costs to provide the necessary continuity? What about the cost to the business if you do not provide that continuity? Do you have financial processes to ensure you are optimising the costs?

- Do you have monitoring and measurement in place to enable proactive measures to assure continuous service?

If you are not able to answer 'Yes' to all or most of these questions, then your organisation may not have adequate arrangements in place to assure the continuity of your business and IT services.

Research within the banking industry, led by the Basel Committee for Banking Supervision, has identified the following risk event types, highlighting the role of IT in these risks:

- fraud – internal and external, such as misreporting information, malicious hacking

- employment practices, such as violation of employee rights and information

- client and business practices, such as misuse of confidential customer information and money laundering

- damage to assets, such as terrorism

- business system failures, such as hardware/software failures and telecommunication/utility outages

- execution and process management, such as data-handling errors and access controls

As a consequence of these findings the Basel Committee produced a paper for the provision of sound practices for managing operational risk (see www.bis.org/bcbs). This paper outlined the need for an appropriate risk management environment; identification, assessment, monitoring and mitigation of risk; the supervisory roles; and the need for disclosure.

These principles are considered throughout this chapter.

5.5 Why is continuity important?

The bottom line for all organisations is to meet their business goals, whether these are financial or non-financial. It is also true to state that the top line has to look at how much it costs to meet those goals and that the processing has to be integrated and end-to-end.

Increasingly, organisations are emphasising that customer satisfaction is the number one imperative for the business, ensuring best practice Service Management.

This requirement exists throughout the whole supply chain and influences decisions relating to the end-to-end service provisioning, introducing joint ventures, partnerships, managed service and outsource options. Naturally these decisions will introduce risk, and be of concern when assuring IT service continuity, especially if insufficient thought is given to how such decisions will be managed by the retained organisation. These issues will be discussed in greater detail in Chapter 7 (Sourcing of IT services).

5.5.1 Management practice

Organisations must genuinely look at the efficiency and effectiveness of the operations that provide the business's products and services. In both public and private organisations they must also ensure that they have adequate internal controls so that they are correctly governed and auditable.

The emphasis is on 'genuine' management, as only too often the management practices are circumvented when the pressure increases. Research by McKinsey and the London School of Economics looked at organisations that had specific management practices, which were rated for the effectiveness of process, performance management of employees, and the calibre of the workforce. These ratings showed that the higher the rating the greater the productivity. This showed that a one-point improvement in rating led to a 25% increase in productivity, which equated to a 5% increase in the return on capital employed (ROCE). This also indicated that if improving management practices without additional IT investment could lead to these increases, then by looking at processes and investing in IT, the organisation gets more 'bang for its buck'!

5.5.2 Efficient and effective processes

The use of IT continues to be a major driver for efficiency and effectiveness, making it more critical to business success and providing opportunity for competitive advantage, increased productivity, transformed working practices and added value to products and services.

Part of the governance requirement now is that the organisation has to be able to prove that it has adequate processes and procedures in place to assure the continuity of the business services. This is audited annually by the relevant regulatory authorities.

Comment

A study in 2003 by the Butler Group identified that investors would be prepared to pay 18% more per share for a company that was proven to have good corporate and IT governance.

5.5.3   Risk management

Most organisations put considerable effort into the design and development of new business services, expending time and costs on getting the solutions that the business needs. However, it is also a regular occurrence for the testing of a new service or a change to be 'cut back', for training to be superficial and for support and maintenance requirements to have not been taken into account.

This only-too-common situation not only places the specific project at risk – it places the quality of the product or service at risk, and in the long term, it could put the business at risk. This is also the situation that has led to increased demands for corporate and IT governance and, through various legislation such as Sarbanes-Oxley and regulations such as Basel II, a need to have to prove compliance.

The fundamental differences of this new thinking are to have an assessment of internal controls and use this to improve business services. It also highlights the importance and necessity for IT in the design, implementation and sustainability of internal control over disclosure and financial reporting. This has placed the requirement to assure service continuity on the Board table, with accountability placed on the Chief Executive Officer (CEO) or Chief Information Officer (CIO).

In a survey of 200 organisations by AMR Research it was reported that almost 60% of the organisations admitted having had coordinated operational risk policies and procedures for less than two years, and 20% still had none.

The pervasive nature of IT and the globalisation of business and service provisioning have increased the risk and therefore the need for risk management. Systems (application, database or Web-based) and networks (voice and data) are integrated and interfaced in a complex manner to provide the business-to-business (B2B) and customer-to-business (C2B) requirements. Additionally, all the internal usage for backroom processing and supporting the business means that any unavailable system or network can have a significant impact on business processing.

While hardware and software failure together form the main cause, human error is responsible for a third of service failures, often because of failings or non-adherence to operating procedures.

5.5.4   Communications

The final aspect that needs to be considered is that of communication. A common complaint by customers of any service is that they do not believe that communications are appropriate. This may be because they cannot find anyone to contact, they do not have a single point of contact or they do not get sufficient updates during the 'incident', and when the issue is resolved they are not told what the cause was. This leads to frustration for the customer. The use of various contact centres has improved some aspects, but may have compounded others if people, process and technology around the communications are not available, timely and accurate.

The use of contact centres has also changed the way the customer gets an initial impression of the business; thus if the services are not available, then the reputation and image of the business are damaged.

IT service continuity, and indeed business continuity as a whole, needs to address all of these issues through the effective provisioning of people, process and technology. With increasing regulation and legislation around the provisioning, this is no longer an option – it is a necessity.

5.6   Who is involved in continuity?

Business and IT service continuity must be part of the overall governance framework for an organisation, and thus are the responsibility of the executives and Board members. However, the activities and processes for continuity must run through the whole organisation.

The Board must set the direction, the policy and the strategy for business continuity. Personnel at lower levels must undertake the necessary actions and act with the necessary diligence to assure continuity, and they must provide the required information to prevent, detect and correct issues around continuity. Within the IT function this is equally, if not more imperative than any other function of the business.

Taking the lead from IT governance, organisations must place overall accountability for service continuity with one specific role; it is suggested that this should be the Chief Information Officer (or that role's equivalent). This means a greater consideration for organisations about whom the Chief Information Officer (CIO) reports to – should this be the Chief Executive Officer (CEO) or the Chief Finance Officer (CFO)? It should not be the Chief Technical Officer (CTO).

The CTO of an organisation may believe that they have built the most resilient infrastructure, have the best resources and have considered all aspects affecting the service. In today's business world and with the criticality of IT to the business, it is essential that they know that the IT operation meets the business needs for reliability, flexibility and consistency.

51

Quote

'I cannot imagine any condition which would cause this ship to founder.'
Captain of the Titanic, 1912

5.6.1 Senior management

Considering these senior roles, at the highest level:

- the Board must take an active role in the defining of mission, policy and strategy for the organisation

- the CEO must introduce a clear organisational structure to support the implementation of the strategy

- the CIO must be business focused and provide a conduit between the business and the IT function

- a steering group should be created with representatives from each executive area to monitor, review and improve the process, people and technical activities

- the Directors/Executives must ensure adherence to policy and strategy, and cascade the individual responsibilities throughout their business unit

- managers must ensure that the discipline of risk and continuity is built into roles and development plans to institutionalise this within the business.

5.6.2 People

Looking at the majority of the personnel that will be involved in assuring continuity, HR policies (and security policy) will need to be reconsidered with regard to personnel.

Comment

If 32% of the causes of IT services failure are human error, how much of this is accidental and how much is malicious? The same could be asked of the software and hardware failures!

Some of the factors in HR that could be of concern for business and IT service continuity include:

- selection – do we perform the necessary checks on the content of applications and on references provided? If the role involves handling sensitive information do we need to do further security checks?

- induction – does the induction of all employees explain the need for governance, security, and risk management?

- training – are all staff correctly trained and do they have the necessary skills to undertake their roles?

- roles and responsibilities – have the responsibilities for activities that form part of business continuity been correctly defined and communicated?

- personal development and objectives – where individuals have specific objectives which need to be set, have these been agreed and recorded within that individual's personal development plan?

- reward and recognition – are there adequate mechanisms in place to maintain morale and motivation within the workforce?

- culture – do the behaviours, attitudes, values and beliefs of the workforce support the requirement for service continuity?

- communication – does the organisation have communication channels that encourage an open and honest working practice?

- leadership and management – does the senior management team provide and demonstrate the necessary leadership for service continuity?

- turnover and mix – is there an unacceptable level of turnover or an imbalance in the ratio of permanent to temporary personnel such that the business is not able to meet the policy requirements for HR and security?

5.7 How do we do it?

5.7.1 Mission

The mission of service continuity is to minimise the business disruption to mission-critical services by taking steps to pre-empt and recover from a variety of business interruptions.

5.7.2 Background

The first activity should be to apply the above mission statement and ensure that it is understood and communicated and that the necessary activities and planning are in place.

5.7.3 Impact assessment

Some fundamental questions are:

- What are the mission-critical services?
- Who says they are the mission-critical services?
- How mission-critical are they?
- What are the components of these services?

- What are the threats to these services and service components?
- What is the likelihood of this threat actually occurring?
- What actions can be taken to mitigate the threats?
- What actions need to be taken to maintain/resume service if the threat becomes reality?
- Who should undertake and manage these actions?
- Are we confident that these actions will meet the requirement?
- In what order should service be restored?
- What actions need to be taken to restore the service back to normal operations?
- What review actions are necessary to prevent reoccurrence?

Again, there are some fundamental questions that help to quickly identify the assets (services, people, process and technology); assess the risks to those assets; identify mitigating actions; undertake mitigating tasks and plan additional continuity actions; test and maintain these plans.

These questions, or the answers to these questions, will also help to ensure that appropriate and proper options analysis and decision-making happens, involving the right people from the business and IT jointly in this process.

The above would be adequate if the services remained at a steady state. However, this is just not realistic, so processes need to be developed that accommodate the project and change activity that is essential within today's business environment, yet protect the need to assure service continuity. This is critical to the principles of asset and Configuration Management.

More detailed information on IT service continuity planning can be found in the ITIL books, *Service Delivery* and *Planning to Implement Service Management*.

5.7.4   Project management

Within the project management framework, it is essential that the requirements for live service are built into the design and development of the solution; that the requirements for operational acceptance are built into the project plan; that effective operational acceptance testing takes place before the service goes live; that a 'go/no go' business decision is built into the implementation plan; and that business and service continuity plans are assessed, amended and tested accordingly.

Many organisations have now developed a 'Gateway' or 'Transition' Team with the responsibility of making sure that production issues are considered when building, testing and implementing new services. These teams pull together the Change, Configuration and Release Management elements defined within the ITIL *Service Support* publication.

5.7.5 Portfolio management

In today's world of IT governance, it is essential that organisations can prove the level of management that is applied to the whole portfolio of work within IT service provision.

Portfolio management does not only mean projects. However, in most organisations it is often the case that there is no one single orchestrated view of what projects are in progress, the status of these projects, the amount of resource utilised and required, and the business justification for these projects.

Without this view, the whole IT service would be deemed to have inherent risk and to be non-compliant.

5.7.6 Change Management

The same disciplines used in project management must be adopted and adapted for the standard Change Management process (see the ITIL *Service Support* book for more detail).

Risk is a standard consideration during the project methodology, but within Change Management it is not always given the same level of serious consideration, and may not have the same level of management commitment.

Consider the 'seven Rs' of Change Management:

1. Who raised the change?
2. What is the reason for the change?
3. What is the return required from the change?
4. What are the risks involved in the change?
5. What resources are required to deliver the change?
6. Who is responsible for the build, test and implementation of the change?
7. What is the relationship between this change and other change?

Without asking and answering all these questions for all changes, the risk element of the change is heightened, and the likelihood that the change will have a detrimental or unexpected impact on the live service is increased.

Many organisations use a simple matrix to categorise risk in terms of high/low impact and high/low probability, and from this the level of change assessment and authorisation required.

An issue with risk assessment is often the subjective nature of the assessment – for example, in the eyes of the developer or support engineer it would always be a high impact, low likelihood risk or a low impact, low likelihood risk. But never forget, the Service Level Agreement (SLA) is the responsibility of the production function, not development.

The 'seven Rs' can be tied into this matrix and used to provide an objective rating, helping us to categorise change better and thus ensure appropriate management.

With Change Management in a complex IT service, it is often the changes that have been categorised as high impact, low likelihood that lead to unexpected change or unavailable service, causing disruption to the business. These changes must have had thorough assessment, wide communication, and appropriate authorisation by the person or persons accountable for that business service.

Within Change Management KPIs also need to be considered for ensuring an effective Change and Configuration Management service.

The single KPI for change must be:

■ the number of changes implemented that met the customer's agreed requirements (expressed as a percentage of all changes).

Naturally there is other management information required around change and statistics to be gathered and analysed to ensure efficient and effective process, but for organisations with a 'dashboard' reporting approach, this is the one metric to use.

5.7.7 Verification and validation

Why does change fail? Invariably this comes down to unsatisfactory verification and validation:

■ verification – doing the right thing
■ validation – doing the thing right.

There is also an element of quality review built into the project and change lifecycles to ensure there is sign-off for key deliverables or at key milestone points, providing authorisation to proceed to the next milestone.

Testing is seen as the stage in a project or change, towards the end of the lifecycle, which is done to ensure that the developers, implementers and supporters will provide the necessary business service. There is some input from users to ensure the functionality of the deliverable.

The testing must also include the operational acceptance of the service or change to ensure it will integrate with other services, will be correctly managed and supported by operations and that adequate arrangements are in place for continuity.

However, testing is almost always 'squeezed' and within testing it is often the operational acceptance elements that are omitted, and with no risk assessment or mitigation. There must be a minimum level of testing. If time is minimal then there must be a mandatory set of tests from an operational perspective. Otherwise how can the IT function assure that it provides a service that meets the SLA?

Without adequate verification and validation, the whole IT service again could now be deemed to have inherent risk and to be non-compliant. Is the CIO (and other Board membership) prepared to accept the consequence?

Acid test

Q1. Do we know what the impact on the business would be if a key service component was unavailable for one week, one day, one hour or one minute?

Q2. Do we have the appropriate Service Management and operational procedures in place to provide the service implied in the answer to Q1?

5.7.8 Monitoring

What are the aspects of service that need to be monitored?

'If it can't be measured it can't be managed.'

There are numerous system management applications being offered that will monitor IT components such as data storage, memory, transactions throughput, temporary buffers and queues, log files and swap space and batch jobs. But from the business perspective the majority of issues with service are around service performance, service availability and deliverables.

Organisations need to reconcile the monitoring of components with the end-to-end service requirements. This means that service providers must identify which components to monitor and measure, what threshold levels to set and what actions to take if those thresholds are breached.

Naturally, the SLA will define the service level targets that have to be monitored, but the service provider must know what to measure and the business implications. How do we identify the events to track, and what automation can be introduced to ensure a rapid and accurate response to those events?

When the system is in the design stage, the analysts should be producing entity models to identify what information needs to be processed. They should also be producing event diagrams to identify the lifecycle of the entity and the information, such as Create, Read, Update and Delete. When the Entity/Event Matrix has been produced this should be used to identify what monitoring needs to be in place after the service is live and also what throughput is expected.

The opposite is also valuable – that is, the operations team can feed into the design production scenarios that can occur to ensure that the service can accommodate these. The risk is being managed and built into the service at the design stage, rather than bolted on at the end of the project.

Once the operations team has the required monitoring it can start to develop the necessary routines and jobs within its Service Management tools. This work should occur during the design and early build stages for the project or change, but invariably this does not happen until late in the build stage at best.

Monitoring and ongoing management and maintenance will also be enhanced by the degree of standardisation that exists in the service architecture. Standardisation enables the service providers to consolidate and optimise infrastructure, not only helping service continuity but also giving better total cost of ownership and governance.

Standardisation will also help with providing an adaptable and reliable platform for business change, and with the provision of the right personnel required to support that service architecture with the right skills.

5.7.9   Leadership

Chapter 2 considered the organisational strategy in detail, but it is worth highlighting the need for good leadership and strong management in governance and risk, and ultimately business and service continuity.

Pressure will be applied to reduce timescales and meet deadlines, to cut budgets and running costs, and to compromise testing. This must not be done without due diligence to governance and risk, and the operational management team will be called upon from time to time to make a 'no go' decision.

Ensuring that there is clear accountability and ownership of this decision and of the affected services will help, and the CIO will have an important role to play. There must be policies and standards defined that make it clear to the internal and external providers what must be done and also what the consequence of non-adherence to policy will be.

Is the loading of illegal software onto the organisation's infrastructure a dismissal offence? How many people have been dismissed for this? This is an area covered by legislation in all countries, with penalties that can be applied to the individual, the management and the business, but only with the introduction of legislation such as Sarbanes-Oxley will this be given the gravity it requires.

5.7.10   Sourcing models

Chapter 7 discusses the various options available for sourcing and partnerships in service provisioning. A fundamental factor in any decision and in defining the contracts must be the continuity of service and the impact on the business.

Organisations that source part or all of their service from external providers must ensure that they have considered the end-to-end service provision, the framework for that provisioning and also that they have effective business and supplier relationship management in place. This is sometimes referred to as the 'Informed Customer'.

The SLA for the service to the business still remains with the internal service provider, underpinned by the contract with the third party. Is the SLA included in the negotiations with the third party, or is this simply left to the procurement team to get 'the best deal'?

6 IT ASSET MANAGEMENT

6.1 Key messages for the Board

IT asset management is about optimising the use and control of IT assets and mitigating related risks. IT assets include software assets as well as the hardware; these may be extremely valuable intellectual property unique to the organisation or standard off-the-shelf packages that have a cost. With the increasing shift to mobile working and more flexible working patterns, it is important to take account of assets used in remote and home working environments away from the office.

6.2 Introduction

There is general consensus that IT delivers value to the business, but few organisations can explain the perceived value of their IT – let alone describe how to improve on it. Few IT departments can easily determine which methods to employ or the metrics to use for measuring the value of IT. They often lack formal methods of communicating with the business to ensure that IT is meeting business need.

IT asset management solves all of these problems. It enables the organisation to:

- understand its current IT and value to the business
- align IT assets with current business objectives
- update IT in line with future business needs and/or exploit opportunities presented by new technology
- control the costs of IT ownership
- meet fiduciary, legal and regulatory requirements in accounting for IT assets.

This chapter explains the principles of IT asset management and the main considerations in managing IT assets.

6.3 IT asset management in context

- Corporate strategy: this determines the current business need for IT assets.
- IT governance: this sets the reporting requirements for management of IT assets.
- Managing change: this identifies changing business need for IT assets.

- Business and service continuity: this ensures that IT assets are resilient enough to ensure that service disruption does not occur.

- Sourcing: this identifies the optimum routes for acquisition of assets.

- Knowledge management: this manages key assets of information and corporate knowledge.

6.4 What is IT asset management?

IT asset management is a set of activities that support strategic or tactical decisions about the organisation's IT assets. This includes acquisition, deployment, disposal or outsourcing of IT capital assets with the aim of achieving appropriate IT capability for the business. It captures information about IT assets, tracks and manages those assets, depreciates the value of the assets over time until disposal of the assets, and identifies changing needs for IT assets. IT asset management is an essential process to enable the organisation to meet its fiduciary, legal and regulatory obligations.

Because IT asset management tracks and monitors the organisation's IT assets, it is a powerful tool for controlling costs and avoiding unnecessary expenditure. It also enables the organisation to assess how well its IT is aligned to current and future business needs.

6.4.1 IT assets

An important aspect of asset management is being able to identify what constitutes an asset. IT assets may be viewed as:

- people (as in experienced IT professionals)
- facilities (buildings)
- equipment (IT hardware, telecommunications)
- software (off-the-shelf or in-house developed).

These assets need to be financially accounted for in a formal way:

- understanding the IT investments that are being made
- recording each IT investment
- knowing when the IT assets are no longer being deployed in the organisation.

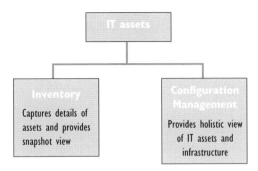

Figure 6.1 – IT asset management

6.4.2 Inventory management

Inventory is a foundational element of asset management. It is often seen as a snapshot in time of the current value of the organisation's assets – quantity and current condition. Auto-discovery tools are a useful aid in identifying the location of IT assets and automating the population of databases with this information.

Some auto-discovery tools are limited to identifying only what they have been programmed to recognise, while other tools may auto-discover all inventory, including authorised as well as unauthorised software. This is a key consideration if licensing is an issue.

Identifying inventory, where it is located, who is using it, how it has changed since last inventoried by using auto-discovery tools can help ensure the quality of the asset information, and allow for more frequent audits of that information.

As staff relocate within the organisation, their IT assets may or may not move with them. Understanding where IT assets are at all times plays a key role in IT asset management. IT asset management enables the IT department to account for assets that are no longer in use, as well as software licences that may no longer be required; this provides additional opportunities to reduce costs.

6.4.3 Configuration Management

The Configuration Management process provides a holistic view of the IT infrastructure, including IT assets used by the business, along with the relationships between those assets. This information is critical for properly determining the risk to the business that may be associated with making changes to the IT infrastructure. Configuration Management data is also useful in recreating the infrastructure following a crisis.

Configuration Management will also inform the IT department in deciding when to update the organisation's current IT.

6.4.4   IT asset management lifecycle

The IT asset management lifecycle defines the key stages in the life of an IT asset. It ensures that the business understands what it needs and that the IT department manages assets to support the business.

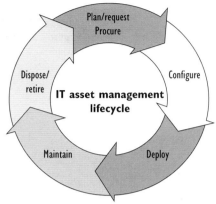

Figure 6.2 – IT asset management lifecycle

The IT asset management lifecycle includes the following activities:

- **plan/request:** this stage should ensure compliance with policy relating to corporate standards. Considerations include: bulk/discount purchasing, simplified maintenance requirements, budgets, technology strategy, business strategy
- **procure:** formal input into inventory and asset management databases
- **configure:** preparation for installation, which will include asset identification (tagging), software readiness, security concerns, remote control software
- **deploy:** physical installation of equipment/software, which includes the asset's location and who is using it
- **maintain:** track any repairs, upgrades, hardware and software patches applied, relocation and redeployment
- **retire:** includes end of life or end of lease. Removes asset from financial records
- **dispose:** physically removing the old assets. Information may include financial costs or compensation.

6.4.5   Maintaining standards

Businesses seeking new technology can be both a blessing and a curse for IT departments. The curse takes effect when the business insists on the latest technology without a real justification for this as part of the request. The IT department has to evaluate and test new software and hardware to ensure that it can function within the current infrastructure without any adverse impacts, such as causing incidents with current systems, requiring updates or upgrades to other systems. As a blessing, businesses that are willing to wait for the evaluation and testing are more willing to accept and value new assets to replace their current ones as part of a planned technology refresh.

The true benefit of asset lifecycle management is the cost saving that the IT department can generate for the business. Through the replacement of IT assets such as hardware on a regular basis, the following benefits can be realised:

- software currency, including latest patches available, which in turn reduces threats and vulnerabilities
- hardware currency, including latest patches, replacement parts available
- reduced maintenance costs (warrant replacement vs. out of warranty replacement)
- retirement of legacy assets means smaller variety of systems for the Service Support personnel to support.

6.5 Why is IT asset management important?

Industry analyst Gartner expects that by 2010, IT spending will represent 50% of most enterprises' capital budget. Without an IT asset management strategy, most large organisations will not be able to achieve strategic cost savings.

A formal IT asset management programme is essential for the planning/request and procurement of assets, and for understanding the value those assets have to the business.

The business value of IT asset management can be demonstrated in the key considerations outlined below.

6.5.1 Cost control

Gartner predicts that by 2010 customers committing at least 3% of their annual operating budgets to formal IT asset management will be likely to achieve a 25% reduction in the total cost of their IT ownership.

With the business looking to IT to reduce budgets and to do more with less, IT management is required to provide return on investment figures and determine the timeframes for new initiatives. The IT department has to be able to show how the organisation's IT aligns with and supports the organisation's financial goals. An effective IT asset management programme helps the IT department to evaluate, measure and analyse the return on investment and potential value to be realised. Detection of under-utilised hardware and software licensing, followed by appropriate remedial action, can justify the costs of IT asset management in a very short period of time.

6.5.2 Software negotiations and compliance

As vendors move to enforce licence agreements, organisations need to be in a position to enforce the terms and conditions that they negotiated in the contracts with their vendors. Many organisations negotiate the contracts well, but are not always diligent in ensuring that they are paying the negotiated rate. The high cost of software, along with the recent changes in software licence models from many vendors has increased the awareness of, and the need for effective software licence management. Unauthorised purchasing of one-off copies of software, lack of software usage information and unauthorised or unlicensed software can have a serious impact on an organisation's IT budget.

Software groups such as the Business Software Alliance (BSA) and Canadian Alliance Against Software Theft (CAAST) report that software piracy amounted to US$30 billion in 2003. As the software industry tries to mitigate losses, industry analysts predict that 40% of medium to large size organisations can expect to be audited by these types of industry groups within the next two years. In the event of an audit, an organisation that lacks competency in managing its software licensing could face punitive fines and penalties.

6.5.3 Regulatory compliance

In recent years, there has been an increase in government regulations such as the Sarbanes-Oxley Act, Health Insurance Portability and Accountability Act, and EU data protection legislation. Compliance with many of these regulations is very difficult without formal IT asset management. An effective IT asset management programme enables the organisation to be fully informed about its hardware, software and service contracts. The organisation can identify which assets it is responsible for, where they are located, the data stored on those assets and who has access to that data. Properly maintained IT asset management ensures that the organisation can be confident about the integrity of information about its IT assets.

6.5.4 Emerging technology

As technology becomes more complex, including increasing use of mobile and portable devices, and the IT needs of the business continue to grow, IT asset managers will need to decide which types of assets warrant tracking, and how best to track them. Without strong IT asset management processes and procedures, this will be a challenging task.

6.5.5 Ensuring IT security

Security is concerned with confidentiality of information, the integrity of the information and its availability. Mitigating security threats to the business has been brought to the forefront in recent years, with the business taking a keen interest. There must be a competent approach to asset disposal with a well-established data eradication process.

Auto-discovery tools can aid in identifying unauthorised software that may be compromising security.

6.5.6   Managing proper disposal of assets

Many IT assets have components that are considered harmful to the environment and therefore must be disposed of in accordance with environmental regulations and guidelines. Security and privacy issues regarding the data storage devices also play a role before equipment can be donated, sold or returned off lease. If a third party is engaged to dispose of the asset, the asset information must be reconciled and data eradication procedures executed. Formal IT asset management, including corporate policies and procedures, will help ensure this is done in accordance with the business's requirements as well as regulatory compliance.

6.5.7   Adapting to changing business needs

In the absence of an IT asset management programme, the business may be ill-equipped to implement strategic business changes. A mature IT asset management process can ease the burden on the IT department in supporting strategic programmes that depart from normal business, as well as atypical occurrences such as mergers and acquisitions. The IT department can provide the business with information about the IT assets. The accountancy function can identify the value of the assets under consideration, in relation to the intended usefulness of the assets. This will assist the business with accurately forecasting their expenses and capital needs, which in turn will directly affect shareholder value. Once IT asset management is operational and effective, the risks and unforeseen costs associated with such business activities can be more accurately budgeted and subsequently reduced.

6.5.8   Reducing financial risk

IT-imposed financial risk can manifest when there is a direct loss of revenue or an unanticipated expense due to poorly timed or poorly planned hardware or software changes, or a system outage. If, for example, an Internet-based payment service's systems experienced extended downtime, business would be halted. Inadequate deployment of IT systems can also contribute to financial risk. For example, an organisation might change to a new customer information system that has not been optimised or sized for the hardware it would be running, thus causing chronic system failures under load. Without a centralised repository detailing the organisation's assets, hardware and software versions, and subsequent upgrades to those systems, the IT department would be hard-pressed to foresee and avoid such risks.

Another important dimension of financial risk is the failure to understand the financial reporting implications of asset change/refresh strategies on the reported financial statements and departmental budgets. Determining net present value (NPV) criteria is generally the key deciding factor in business case assessment. However, there are other political aspects that must be considered, especially in publicly traded organisations.

6.5.9 Reducing legal risk

There are legal risks related to software piracy, non-compliance with software licence agreements, copyright infringements and improper disposal of electronic equipment. Organisations that fail to comply with the regulations governing these events may face fines and/or their senior management may face criminal prosecution. The possibility that their public image and brand are damaged can harm (often irreparably) customer confidence and spur customer defection. IT asset management is important in minimising licensing risk.

IT asset management's true value lies in its long-term ability to optimise the use and control of IT assets and mitigate related risks. IT asset management can be justified based on its ability to control costs and make deals. However, its long-term payback lies in its ability to effectively facilitate both technical and organisational change, and to make tactical and strategic decisions about the organisation's overall IT and the level of risk it is willing to assume.

6.6 Organisation, roles and responsibilities

6.6.1 Considerations for the organisation of IT asset management

IT asset management must be coordinated across the organisation. It may be appropriate to centralise the function to realise its greatest potential. However, decentralisation should also be considered. This is especially important in larger organisations with multiple divisions or units that span many locations.

Effort should be made to centralise the following areas because of their strategic nature:

- strategic IT planning:
  - use of standardised IT architectures
  - use of standardised products
  - rationalisation of software and hardware deployment
- strategic sourcing (software and hardware):
  - centrally negotiated pricing reflecting total purchasing power
  - time-phased requirements
- risk management:
  - legal compliance, including management of relationships with auditors, authorities and compliance organisations
  - management of the impact of unexpected events on the organisation, e.g. licensing audits

- software licence control and distribution for the entire organisation
- coordination of the reallocation of software licences and hardware asset between business units, e.g. facilitating the redeployment of licences from units with excess, to those with growing needs.

The following operational functions are good candidates for decentralisation, as they are not strategic:

- procurement processing
- deployment and installation
- operation and maintenance of the detailed IT asset management (or Configuration Management) database including physical proof for software licences.

6.6.2 Roles and responsibilities

For IT asset management to succeed within an organisation, it is important that roles and responsibilities are clearly defined and agreed, and that the scope of ownership of each of the processes is also defined and agreed. These roles and responsibilities should be adapted to fit the individual requirements of each organisation in accordance with its size, structure and geographical distribution. In small organisations, these roles could be combined, with one or two individuals performing most of these roles. The primary roles are outlined below.

- **Management sponsor:** there must be sponsorship and commitment from senior managers both within the business and the IT department. This will ensure that the visibility of IT asset management is maintained and that the organisational culture is developed to enable the IT asset management processes to succeed. It will facilitate the request for sufficient budget and resources. Management sponsorship and commitment must be maintained and not be allowed to deteriorate.

- **Configuration manager:** this is the person with overall responsibility for the Configuration Management process. This includes much of the scope of IT asset management.

- **IT asset manager:** this individual should be responsible for the management of all IT assets within an organisation. They would have overall responsibility for establishing and maintaining the IT asset database. (This is logically part of the Configuration Management Database (CMDB), even if physically separate.) This database should also contain all of the information required by IT asset management processes.

- **IT asset management process owner:** in some organisations, responsibility for the overall effectiveness and efficiency of IT asset management processes rests with the IT asset management process owner. This role is basically responsible for ensuring that a continual process of improvement is applied to all IT asset management (ITAM) processes.

- **Asset analysts or configuration librarians:** these are responsible for maintaining up-to-date (and historical) records of IT assets including software version control.

- **Procurement or purchasing advisors:** the department responsible for procurement and/or purchasing has principal responsibility for managing all aspects of IT procurement as well as the end-user organisation, with guidance to the extent necessary from IT management and personnel.

- **Legal advisors:** responsible for the provision of legal advice and guidance, contractual issues and legal matters.

- **Change manager:** ensures that an effective Change Management process is in place to control all changes within the IT infrastructure.

6.7 How to manage IT assets

6.7.1 Key issues

- Concentrate on issues by targeting the problem areas
- Plan ahead for process and data integration of new functions
- Ensure objectives are clearly communicated, successes are advertised
- Ensure that processes support improved data integrity.

Understand that data accuracy will take time to achieve; identify the data that is important in the short term. Data may not be accurate or useful immediately. It will need to be validated before it is trusted and of real use to the organisation. Concentrate your efforts on the key data that can be used to manage the most significant problem areas.

6.7.2 Critical success factors

- To ensure IT asset management's strategic role in the organisation and future directions is sustained, establish sponsorship and ownership of IT asset management with a senior executive.

- Implement a single asset database to ensure compliance and compatibility is maintained throughout the organisation.

- Establish centralised management of IT asset management practice to ensure that compliance and compatibility throughout the organisation is maintained and that asset management is incorporated into the organisation's strategic plans.

- To ensure that the integrity of the asset management data is maintained, integrate asset management with all IT management practices. This should be an accepted part of other processes that originate changes such as on-site support, application development, network services and human resources.

- To ensure efficient and effective operation of IT asset management and to ensure the integrity of the data, serious consideration should be given to implementing support tools such as enterprise management software, software distribution tools, software metering and monitoring tools that integrate with the asset management database.

- To ensure the asset management process can be measured, managed and improved, establish metrics to record and analyse the performance of asset management.

6.7.3 Key IT asset management questions for the Board

- Who is responsible for knowing the legal obligations for corporate assets and liabilities?

- How are your assets valued and is this information accurate? How is this information stored? Is there appropriate backup of this information from your IT department?

- When costing assets, do you consider the following to determine total cost of ownership:
  - procurement costs?
  - deployment costs?
  - usage costs?
  - contract costs?
  - support costs?
  - retirement costs?
  - continuity requirements?

- What are the contingency plans in terms of loss of asset and how often are the high-risk items reviewed? Who is responsible? Does IT have appropriate backups and Configuration Management allowing you to source adequate replacements? Who is responsible for the quality review of this information?

- Do you understand the correlation between IT assets and the business functions and services they support?

- Do you have standards in place for procurement and deployment of assets? If not, what are the implications for:
  - interoperability?
  - architecture?
  - security?
  - archiving?

- Can your organisation produce current licences for all software that resides on its servers? What about desktops and laptops?
- What is the number of machines in your environment?
    - What about wireless devices?
    - How much is your organisation spending to support and maintain them?
- Are tools in place to adequately track and manage assets and are they accurate?
- Are processes effective and consistent?
- Is there organisational buy-in to actively manage the IT environment and optimise IT?
- Are the timelines and goals you have set for your IT asset management programme realistic, and are they aligned to business needs?

6.7.4   IT asset management checklist

The following checklists should be used to help to define all aspects of IT asset management.

Strategic aspects

IT asset management plays a key role in strategic planning. Key components to consider include:

- organisational buy-in to actively manage the IT environment
- tools in place to adequately track and manage assets
- defined policies for IT asset management
- established and consistently implemented processes
- IT asset management aligned to business needs.

Cost of ownership:

- purchase
- prepare and deploy
- maintenance/contracts
- contingency/disaster recovery
- retire/disposal.

Value of IT asset management database:

- software licensing auditable
- all assets tracked throughout their lifecycle (from procurement to disposal)
- ties to accounting to accurately depreciate the asset.

Tactical

From a tactical standpoint, key policies need to be established and adopted throughout the organisation.

Asset policies:

- plan/request
- procurement
- configuration
- deployment
- maintenance
- relocation of assets
- redeployment
- decommissioning
- end of life
- disposal.

Risk:

- responsibilities established for legal obligations for corporate assets and liabilities
- defined contingency plans in terms of loss of asset
- high risk items reviewed on a regular basis
- business continuity responsibility is assigned and understood (see Chapter 5).

Operational

Consider the need for tools used to support the IT asset management process. Smaller organisations may well be able to manage and control the asset information using non-automated means. Larger organisations will require significant overhead to successfully meet the minimum requirements for successful IT asset management, if tools and automation are not adopted.

Tools:

- asset management
- procurement tracking
- financial allocation
- inventory and auto-discovery.

7 SOURCING OF IT SERVICES

7.1 Key messages for the Board

IT is becoming increasingly complex, with a constant mix of disparate, rapidly changing technologies. Sourcing of IT services can increase the organisation's IT capability and help to stabilise costs.

7.2 Introduction

Sourcing decisions are all about deciding the mix of internal and external service provision – that is, which elements of an IT service should be provided internally, externally or even shared with others.

This chapter presents a complete overview of the importance of making appropriate IT sourcing decisions to support the business, and then managing the contracts and working relationships associated with those services for business results.

7.3 What is sourcing?

7.3.1 Sourcing

Sourcing is the process of seeking alternatives to performing IT operational and business activities internally. It generally entails contracting with IT service providers to provide these services for a fee via an agreed contract covering cost and conditions (e.g. service levels).

There are many different models of sourcing. For example:

- the customer retains strategy for IT direction setting
- the customer wants to have the third party set all IT direction but they must migrate the current IT staff to the third-party supplier. This ensures some business-specific knowledge is transferred to the third-party supplier
- the customer wants to outsource only a portion of the IT environment, e.g. desktop, because it is expensive and a third-party supplier can do it better and will refresh the technology more often.

7.3.2   Partnering

Partnering exists when two or more companies develop a close relationship to attain specific business objectives. It is not the same as a partnership, such as the model used by legal firms. The aim of partnering is to maximise the effectiveness of each partner's resources, in a relationship that is characterised by mutual openness and trust within a commercial arrangement. Most partnering agreements are long-term in nature. For partnering to be effective, clients must work with suppliers to establish agreed goals and parameters. A formal measurement system should also be created and used to track progress towards agreed objectives. For example:

- major automobile makers such as Ford and General Motors have mature arrangements with suppliers that use 'two-way' performance evaluations, which require suppliers to initiate improvement programmes when they get deficient reviews

- Maytag Appliances shares savings with key suppliers through a relationship that uses a 50/50 savings split to incentivise and commit them to continuous improvement programmes.

There are many concerns that drive an organisation to consider sourcing options. Management is looking to save money or take advantage of the latest technology without major investment. They also want IT staff in place where their primary focus is IT and customer support. Reducing cost does play a large role but is not always the overriding driver.

Today the major area where sourcing and partnering occurs is in IT, followed closely by administrative functions (between 35% and 50% of sourcing contracts). Human resources, distribution, facilities management, finance, manufacturing and call centres range between 10% and 20% (frequently referred to as business process outsourcing).

7.4   Why sourcing options are important

Listed below are the key reasons that organisations have identified to consider sourcing.

- **Reduce and control operating costs**
  Benefit: An external provider's lower cost structure, which may be the result of a greater economy of scale or other advantage based on specialisation, reduces the organisation's operating costs and increases its competitive advantage.

  Risk: Reliance on an external provider reduces the organisation's ability to directly control costs and leaves it at the mercy of the provider's financial strategy as well as market influences.

- **Improve organisation focus**

  Benefit: Outsourcing enables the organisation to focus on its core business by having non-core functions assumed by an external expert.

  Risk: The organisation does not have direct control of its IT expertise; it is exposed because the provider is responsible for management of the expertise and skill sets.

- **Gain access to world-class skills**

  Benefit: World-class providers make extensive investments in technology, methodologies and people. This combination of specialisation and expertise gives customers a competitive advantage. In addition, there are better career opportunities for personnel who make the transition to the outsourcing provider.

  Risk: If a skill is in short supply the provider may not be able to make the skill sets available to all customers as required.

- **Free up internal resources**

  Benefit: Outsourcing allows the organisation to redirect key people (or at least the staff roles they represent) on to greater value-adding activities.

  Risk: Key people may choose not to work for the provider and still leave the organisation.

- **Shared risk**

  Benefit: Outsourcing and partnering make investments on behalf of many clients, which spreads corporate risk. High risks are associated with the IT investments an organisation makes.

  Risk: Markets, competition, government regulations, financial conditions and technologies all change rapidly; sharing of risks may only help in specific areas.

The benefits realised from improving customer and service provider relationships can be highly significant in terms of quality of service and better value for money for both the IT department and internal business customers. It also provides an opportunity for service providers to gain a better understanding of customer needs, which enhances long-term relations.

7.5 Organisation, roles and responsibilities

7.5.1 Organisational prerequisites

- The strategic context for decisions about sourcing, the business reasons for going to the sourcing and partnering model should be well defined.

- There should be a framework for guidance and regulation of sourcing arrangements.

- Formal approaches to managing change enable the business to manage the dynamics of provider relationships.

- A comprehensive approach to business continuity takes account of new risks that might be introduced through sourcing arrangements.

- The concept of intellectual property and information can be blurred when engaged in sourcing; new approaches to controlling 'knowledge' must be addressed and in place.

- A Service Level Management process must be in place to define/monitor Service Level Agreements (SLAs) and underpinning contracts.

7.5.2 Customer and organisational roles

These include:

- 'Informed Customer'

- the purchasing relationship (procurement)

- non-purchasing relationships (managing the contract and working relationship).

7.5.3 Responsibilities

OGC's *IT Supplier Code of Best Practice* identifies and details 10 commitments (i.e. responsibilities) needed to support a customer–supplier relationship. A copy of this Best Practice code can be found at the following website: www.ogc.gov.uk/embedded_object.asp?docid=1004859

7.6 Implementation of sourcing and partnering

Not all organisations are ready for sourcing or partnering. The organisation must look at its overall culture. The following questions are examples of general issues to be addressed when considering sourcing.

- How would sourcing and partnering be perceived within the organisation? If it is viewed in an overly negative context then time must be spent evaluating the risk of alienating key resources.

- How successful is the organisation in managing service providers and contracts? If past history shows a gap or poor results in the past where providers needed to be managed then time must be spent to build expertise. The worst time to develop contract negotiation skills is during negotiations!

- How mature is the organisation? If it does not have established, mature process-driven Service Management (e.g. ITIL Service Management) then it should focus on developing these processes before considering sourcing.

7.6.1 How to approach sourcing

Before engaging in sourcing/partnering arrangements, an organisation must first exercise 'due diligence' in assessing whether sourcing/partnering is right for the organisation; it must develop a sourcing/partnering strategy. This can be done internally or by consulting specialist experts for their advice.

A pre-sourcing activity consists of:

- clear motivation (what are the drivers?)
- identifying core competencies
- understanding the organisation's assets
- market scan (who is doing what?)
- sourcing/partnering case studies relative to your type of business
- determining what different delivery channels offer
- risk analysis
- defining quality and how to measure business benefits
- defining what success will be and how to measure it.

7.6.2 Stages of a sourcing project

There are five stages to a sourcing project:

- determining the business need and the market's capability to meet that need
- developing a procurement strategy
- identifying and selecting suitable providers and finalising a contract to deliver the service or services
- transition – implementing a new service or services including setting up the governance arrangements for working with the new provider
- ongoing management of the service contract and working relationship.

This is a simplified view of the process of sourcing. In practice, there may be multiple providers and/or shared arrangements with other customers to consider.

Note that public sector organisations must comply with strict procurement rules when sourcing external IT services. OGC provides comprehensive guidance on procurement for UK public sector bodies.

Critical success factors for sourcing projects

- **Planning:** IT Service Management must be included as part of the 'Plan-Do-Check-Act' cycle as required by management system standards such as ISO/IEC 20000.
- **Teams:** create a designated team that has ownership of the sourcing initiative.
- **Control:** formalise all aspects of controls (physical, security, transaction and continuity).
- **Performance:** create, monitor and use SLAs so that exceptional performance is rewarded and poor performance is discouraged. Productivity of sourcing must also be tied to the organisation's overall performance reporting structure.
- **Knowledge transfer:** formalise the approach to maintaining the transfer of core knowledge so that the service provider is kept up to date with changes and transitions to process. This can include a training component as well.
- **Risk analysis:** review risk at the beginning and then periodically so that the direction of the sourcing initiative maintains stability.
- **Post-implementation review:** conduct an analysis to determine success of the project and what lessons can be learned.

It is good practice to have some form of *Management Gates:* these are management reviews that take place at the end of each stage and act as 'reality checks' before the project is allowed to proceed to the next stage. These gates should be designed to verify/control budgets, identify any dramatic scope changes and assess whether the risks outweigh the project's worth.

7.6.3   The need for an integrated toolset

A structured management framework should be used to control any sourcing arrangement. Best practice such as ITIL provides process control and integration that can easily adapt to a sourcing initiative. New toolsets that support the ITIL framework are also available so that the management of sourcing arrangements can be automated and better controlled. When considering these tools, the integration of processes and tools across the supply chain also needs to be addressed. A data architect needs to identify control data that has to be aligned or mapped with the tool.

In an ITIL environment, the Service Level Management process will identify, record and manage the SLAs that must be created to manage sourcing arrangements. The Configuration Management Database will be the repository for the SLAs. The Incident Management function as well as Change Management must have access to the SLAs so that incidents and changes can be managed with regard to the sourcing. All of these processes can be integrated via a single tool/application so that the SLA information is seamless, easily managed and available on demand. These tools provide instant awareness of the sourcing performance and status of sourcing relationships. This reporting capability is indispensable when managing and governing sourcing arrangements.

Before selecting Service Management tools determine which organisation is going to be ITIL aligned. If you are expecting the service provider to be ITIL aligned, then as the customer you want to establish the SLAs and reports so that you are receiving the benefits of a provider whose operational model is ITIL aligned. In this scenario you would let the provider choose the integrated toolset. If you are retaining some IT provision internally, and the external provider is only performing one role within the IT environment, then you would want to choose the integrated toolset and establish the appropriate data feeds from your external provider.

7.6.4 Handling interdependencies within sourcing

The organisation should have identified all interdependencies related to the sourcing during Stage 1 (identifying the business need). The interactions between these dependencies will be accounted for during planning in Stage 4 (transition). An integrated tool will help to support these interdependencies during the sourcing transition.

The following are examples of some of the interdependencies that can exist in a sourcing relationship:

- *transition of data* to sourcing systems – initially address core data that needs to be synchronised, valid and on time, but be prepared to expand the scope. The sourcing arrangement may demand extensive information flows across the organisational boundaries

- *financial transactions* – end of month/year closing dates and requirements must be identified and supported by the service provider

- *skills* – unique, organisation-specific skills need to be communicated, trained for and updated

- *security* requirements – the service provider must be kept up to date with any changes to security

- *system* requirements – any hardware requirement changes must be conveyed to the service provider early on

- *compliance* – areas such as Sarbanes-Oxley and CobiT need to be understood and addressed by the service provider relative to the needs of the business so that the sourcing operation is auditable/compliant at all times.

7.6.5 Linking of sourcing activities throughout the organisation

In Stage 4 planning, the sourcing strategy is mapped across the organisation. This is where the budget is tied to the financial group, services are tied to the Service Delivery group, security considerations are tied to the security group, etc. Each group that is linked to the sourcing initiative must make provisions for interaction with the service provider so that the sourcing operation will continue to run smoothly. These links should be tested during each phase of the implementation process to verify that the link is working and providing the correct transaction between the business and the service provider.

For example, if the business wants to update the security software on the systems that the service provider is using to run the business's financial information, the security group should have an established contact with the service provider to convey this need.

If the service provider needs to increase the business-specific skill level of a new employee, they should have an established contact with the training department of the business and/or specialist experts within the organisation.

Every aspect of the sourcing operation as it pertains to the business it supports must be linked to the appropriate area/group within the business. If these links are not identified and established early on, the sourcing relationship will not be efficient and will have many bottlenecks that will affect productivity. For example, if an organisation depends on a supply chain, then the supply chain must be clearly linked to the sourcing activity. One of the best ways to map and control the alignment is by using the Service Level Management process (i.e. though SLAs and underpinning contracts).

7.6.6   Interfacing sourcing activities to Service Management

The best approach to interfacing sourcing to Service Management is through a direct link to the organisation's Service Desk. The scope of interfacing the sourcing initiative to the Service Desk should take place during the strategy and implementation planning stages. If Service Desk rules exist for functions that are being sourced they may be reused (i.e. the rules will have to be rewritten so that the sourcing perspective is captured).

For example, if a sourced application goes 'down', there must be details in the Configuration Management Database that allow groups such as the Service Desk to know where the application was running and who is responsible so that the Incident Management process can engage the right level of support in the right area. If support is still handled by the business, then they must be given the correct information so they can locate the system. If the service provider is responsible for keeping the application running, then the Service Desk must be able to match an SLA to the sourced application and start monitoring the down-time relative to the agreed service level.

This scenario is similar for all of the Service Management processes. Enough time must be spent during scope investigation and planning of the sourcing arrangement to map/document the interaction that needs to occur between the sourcing arrangement and all of the Service Management functions.

7.6.7 Measuring success

There are many different ways to monitor sourcing initiatives. Two aspects for measuring sourcing arrangements are through monitoring the sourcing implementation and monitoring the ongoing performance of operations (sometimes called maintenance monitoring). Each has a different perspective and focus.

Implementation monitoring: this measures how well the transition and migration to the sourcing is progressing. A detailed project plan should be used to guide the transitions with milestones and assessments at every key stage of sourcing. Migration must be done in phases to reduce the impact of a massive disruption to the business. As each function is taken over by the service provider, it must be tested for quality and verified that the 'sourced' function meets the negotiated SLAs associated with the process. Exception reporting must be reviewed with the service provider and action taken before another phase of the implementation can start. Implementation monitoring will continue until the implementation is completed.

> **Examples of implementation monitoring**
>
> - Were key milestones met?
> - Were costs on target?
> - Was the predicted return on investment delivered?

Performance monitoring: this is an ongoing process that continuously monitors the sourced functions. It needs to be put in place after the implementation has occurred. This type of monitoring usually involves weekly or monthly status reporting with monthly management reviews and quarterly performance review meetings with service providers. Exception reporting must be addressed by the service provider, with corrective action and/or penalties. Sourcing performance monitoring should be integrated with the overall business reporting functions.

Both these aspects of monitoring should be automated so that key resources are totally focused on the problems/exceptions and not on data collection. A relationship management team with extensive negotiating skills would be ideal for this type of process. The people involved in the Service Level Management process should be included in these activities to support the relationship management team.

7.6.8 Performance measurements and auditing

The sourcing contract should specify clear Service Level Agreements as well as key performance indicators (KPIs). KPIs should be designed to measure the performance of the service provider. For example, the SLAs and KPIs should work together for an outsourced Incident Management process. The SLA sets a target for incidents that were resolved during first level support and the KPI measures/reports the actual percentage of incidents that were resolved during first level support over a designated period of time. It is the responsibility of the business to make sure these levels are met. Two perspectives are needed – past performance and predicting what will happen in the future.

Past performance is the current level of performance. This is needed to establish a baseline and to help create new targets and levels to drive to. The baseline should not only be internal but should also reflect what is occurring in similar organisations – benchmark against other organisations similar to yours to determine appropriate costs and performance levels.

Predicting performance is about the future. You will need to create a model from existing performance data and predict what should be expected as the sourcing continues. Benchmarking is not a one-time exercise but an ongoing process. Periodically compare costs and performance levels with your counterparts.

In both cases it is prudent to use an independent third-party organisation to conduct the audit to eliminate any subjectivity that might occur. Negotiations should ensue if the results show that your organisation is no longer close to the market norm in pricing and/or performance.

Benchmarking, monitoring and measurements should be used to give providers incentives to improve. These can also be used to discourage poor performance, but that approach has a tendency to diminish the trust in a partnering relationship and in many cases will initiate the demise of the sourcing engagement. The benchmarking should be used as a tool to tune the sourcing engagement, allowing both sides to find the happy medium and garner success.

The use of Balanced Scorecards is recommended as the best way to report on performance. The detail and content of these reports is related to the audience that will receive the reports.

- Weekly status reports should go to the project leaders and managers. They should contain KPI status as well as alerts of any changes/possible changes that may have an adverse affect on the engagement.

- Project data and metrics reports should be monthly or twice monthly with enough detail to measure all the key processes covered by the sourcing engagement. Trend lines should be derived from these reports as soon as enough statistical data has been collected.

- Project monitoring reports should be created on a monthly basis showing a high-level view of the project so that any exposure/adverse occurrence will stand out. These reports should go to the Board for review.

The relationship management group should meet once a month to review all the reports and make recommendations to the Board with regard to actions to be taken. These actions can range from 'business as usual' to renegotiation of sourcing contracts. The Steering Board will have the final approval of the actions.

Figures 7.1 to 7.4 represent examples of four different types of dashboard reports that might be used to show the relationships between measurements.

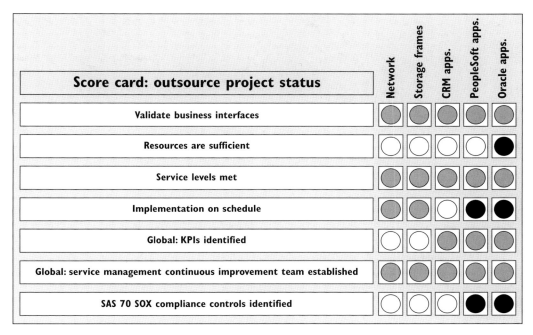

Figure 7.1 – Management reporting (example A)

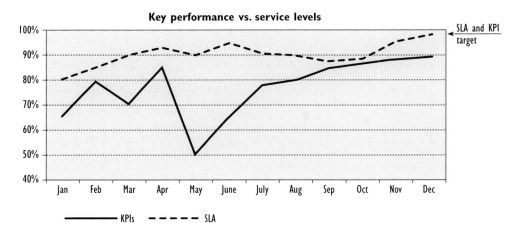

Figure 7.2 – Management reporting (example B)

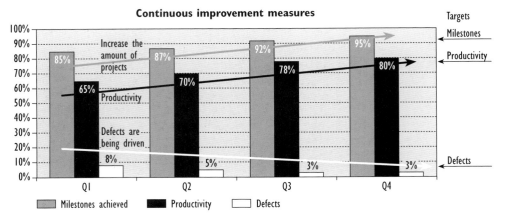

Figure 7.3 – Management reporting (example C)

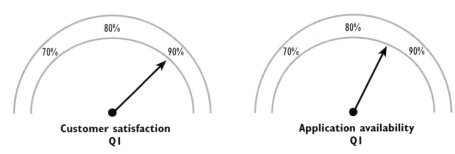

Figure 7.4 – Management reporting (example D)

Example case study: sourcing a Service Desk

In 2004 a North American-based manufacturing company decided to outsource its Service Desk. The due diligence was accomplished in about three months and the transition was initially scheduled to take six months. The project encompassed two radical changes – from in-house to offshore outsource support and switch to a completely different Service Desk tool. Due to cost and business drivers the implementation was accelerated and the rollout was reduced to two months. The original project failed to meet the success criteria within the time constraints, the service provided was unsatisfactory and the businesses that used the Service Desk were very unhappy. It took another 12 months to finally fix the problems but by then the damage was done and the business units looked very unfavourably on the IT unit from then on.

Questions that the business must ask

Q1. Is the projected long-term impact to your business (e.g. cost, culture change, risk, etc.) justified by the ROI you expect to realise from a sourcing or partnering arrangement?

Q2. Do you have the appropriate Service Management and operational procedures in place to support sourcing or partnering (i.e. does the proposed solution have an ITIL Service Management model embedded in the solution)?

Q3. Do you know what the impact on business would be if you had to back out of a sourcing or partnering agreement?

Q4. Have all major risks to your business in relation to the sourcing/partnering initiative been identified, planned for and/or mitigated?

Q5. Do you have the appropriate performance monitoring and scorecard reporting in place to support sourcing or partnering?

8   KNOWLEDGE MANAGEMENT

8.1   Key messages for the Board

Knowledge management is concerned with managing information in context. Today, knowledge management is not confined within the organisation. Knowledge has to be managed across networks outside the organisation. Relationships with customers are changing – for example, in the newly merged UK Inland Revenue and HM Customs and Excise, which now has a much more complete picture of its customer base. Accountability for customer information is a concern for both public and private sector organisations. Privacy of data is very important today from the governance and compliance perspectives. Finally, the IT infrastructure must be an enabler – not a barrier – for knowledge management across a community network.

8.2   Introduction

Are all of your information assets, electronic and paper, under proper and appropriate control?

Does a culture of collaboration and communication exist in your organisation that ensures information is available to those that need it in a timely and effective way?

Are corporate knowledge services (for example, Service Desks) centred on good practice principles that support storage and retrieval of information in a way that serves the business to the optimum?

Do you understand the risk of being unable to access information in the event of major IT failures?

Is knowledge management a technology issue?

These questions and more are addressed in the following pages.

Knowledge management has been described as many things, from managing ignorance to managing intellectual property. It is more a set of guiding principles in many senses, with the underlying tenet of information in context.

Without context, information has little value. Largely, people think about things they know and can discuss because they can place them in context, either because of experience or education. To provide an example, if 'e = mc²' is shown to an audience, *nearly* everyone who has gone through even rudimentary science education will be aware that a scientist called Einstein was involved somewhere and the equation alludes to a major breakthrough in scientific thought; a significant proportion will be able to put this into the context of 'the theory of relativity' and some scientists will be able to explain the whole thing. Anyone who hated science subjects and avoided the classes may well find the letters to be completely meaningless.

The point is that all knowledge is shaped by context and everyone relies on education and experience to make sense of it; the sense they make of it (or put another way, the depth of understanding) differs from person to person, depending on their education and experience. Communities of users with a specific interest or requirement are a key element in creation and dissemination of knowledge, and though they are not the reason for a knowledge environment, they provide focus and energy.

8.3 Knowledge management in context

8.3.1 Knowledge management and corporate strategy

Several years ago at Montgomery Watson Harza (MWH), knowledge management was associated with IT. But contrary to popular belief, having knowledge management activities reside in IT did not alienate employees or leave them with a bad taste in their mouths; it left them with no taste at all. As Victor Gulas, Chief Knowledge Officer of MWH puts it, 'At that point knowledge management was not very visible. People thought, "I don't see anything. It doesn't impact me." Now that we have brought it to a more strategic level, employees are starting to notice a visible impact and a place for them.'

Given that IT is a major component of any modern corporate strategy, how can knowledge management help solve the perceived problems of aligning the corporate strategy with IT? The first area is the understanding of the role of IT. Being informed about IT at Board level is important. But understanding how to exploit IT as an enabler and knowing also how to avoid the usual pitfalls of over-budgeting and underachievement is the key.

8.3.2 Knowledge management and governance

Do you know what you know? This may appear facetious, but knowing what you know is at the root of corporate governance. The financial scandals of recent times came to light when auditors discovered anomalies in what was known (or in some cases hidden). A knowledge culture would not have stopped the actions that led to the crises, but it would have arrested the development of the crises much earlier.

Today, organisations have to ensure adequate privacy and confidentiality of data to meet the requirements of customers and regulators. In shared services arrangements (such as consolidated delivery centres) it is increasingly important to ensure that knowledge is not 'leaked' from one service provider to another; additional measures and controls may be needed to protect privacy and confidentiality. In order to comply with legislation or corporate policies, the organisation must be aware of the contextual issues within which it is operating. Executives can make the most of their contribution by leading from the front, asking the right questions and encouraging appropriate behaviours. Too often, executives are content to allow subordinates to take the blame for their own failure to address knowledge gaps or their own failure to take responsibility where corporate knowledge has not been adequately communicated.

8.3.3   Knowledge management and managing change

Knowledge management is an essential component of business change. The cultural issues that militate against organisational change are in most respects identical with those that challenge the institution of a knowledge culture. Moving from the position that change is bad, to change is good, is culturally the same as embracing knowledge sharing rather than 'information is power' mentality!

Figure 8.1 illustrates different types of change.

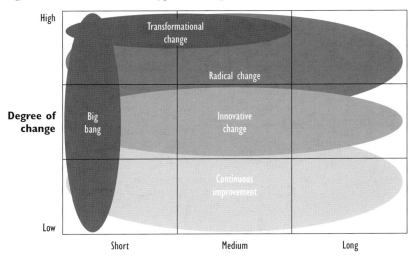

Figure 8.1 – Different types of change

Business transformation is defined here as:

> '... the translation of policies and objectives into the desired outcomes through the radical redesign of relevant aspects of the business.
>
> The desired result is an improved capability to deliver better public services and/or major efficiency improvements.'

People use the same words to mean different things; radical, transformational and 'big bang' change are often used indiscriminately. The issue is that irrespective of description, managing a corporate change requires knowledge, not just islands of disconnected information.

In all spending reviews, UK government departments have been called upon to support a significant reduction in the cost of structural government. Most of the savings are being sought through improvements in internal efficiency – that is, lower investments in resources will be expected to go further and generate the same or greater output. Many departments will only be able to achieve the required level of improvements through radical and transformational change of their business processes. There is greater scope for efficiency savings by harmonising or integrating back office functions across commercial and government organisations. And every one of these corporate changes requires investment in knowledge and investment in cultural change that in turn is brought about by investment in a knowledge culture.

8.3.4 Knowledge management and continuity of service

When the World Trade Center was hit on 9/11, it became apparent very soon that those companies with the people and processes available to manage their knowledge fared much better in the aftermath than those that had not invested in knowledge management.

The knowledge was not technical (though technical knowledge was needed to rebuild the IT); it was the knowledge to put businesses back into operational service as quickly as possible; how staff could be relocated and remain effective; how to use extranets when information is needed; and how much knowledge about skills and support had been overlooked.

8.3.5 Knowledge management and assets

The question *Do you know what you know?* can equally be applied here. Executives do not have to be capable of quoting every asset in their remit; however, they should be capable of knowing who in their organisation is responsible for all IT assets, all financial data, all HR data, all audit data – in fact all knowledge in the organisation.

Of course, the most effective way to achieve this is to make someone accountable for knowledge management in the organisation. Many UK police authorities have been active in recruiting knowledge management teams, not just nominating the nearest manager for the role.

The police forces have realised that their intelligence is better served collectively than individually. 'Joining up' information sources, creating communities and using information as a key asset are major drivers for the future.

8.3.6 Knowledge management and sourcing/partnering

Last in this section is the link to sourcing and partnering. If you have no knowledge of the value of outsourcing or the cost of partnering or perhaps the performance of those you wish to do business with, how will you know if any sort of deal is worth pursuing?

8.4   Why is knowledge management an executive issue?

Can an enormous international coalition of intelligence agencies gather appropriate contextual data to inform strategic government decisions? How will governments manage information flow to the public as legislation such as Freedom of Information and Data Protection regulations begin to bite? As a more mobile workforce moves jobs more frequently how will business continuity, ethos and culture be maintained?

Understanding where knowledge and information flows is key to success. Computers can mine gargantuan databases to establish patterns and throw up information that a human could never find in several lifetimes. The most advanced artificial intelligence is still, however, no substitute for what has been described as 'the human glue' that provides context and allows inferences to be accurately – or inaccurately – made.

Libraries are the old-fashioned knowledge repositories. However, the principles of managing that repository are as valid today as they were 100 years ago. Who better to understand the need to organise, index and maintain massive databases than librarians? Long-term productivity depends on both investment and growth of knowledge assets. Joining up information flows, identifying and eradicating duplication of effort, streamlining data collection and distribution; all these things are crucial to managing an efficient productive organisation and all are enabled by managing information, *knowledge*, as an asset.

Figure 8.2 illustrates the four facets of knowledge management that must be addressed (and some of the reasons why they must be addressed) in a generic form recognisable to the majority of organisations.

Culture: issues to consider include the corporate culture and any changes that are required from the executive. Culture is led from the top of the office, thus if a 'centre of excellence' is required then the Board will demonstrate commitment through investment and interest in change initiatives. Consider aspects that may be of concern to the workforce such as flexible working and how control is exercised when the organisation is geographically separated (perhaps geography determines some cultural separation too).

Behaviour: culture often determines behaviour. If there is a culture of 'us and them' then 'silo' working becomes normal and entrenched. If communications are poor, perhaps technology or process can help, but is the culture one of openness and team working?

Process: process control can be central or local; often it is vitally important that control is exercised in a repeatable, auditable manner, but is it always necessary to control every process centrally? Take a view on mandatory and desirable policies that will help you in creation of the culture and behaviours you wish to encourage.

Technology: websites, intranets, the overall e-presence of your organisation are all based on technology choices. Have all the choices been consistent? Is the technology providing the

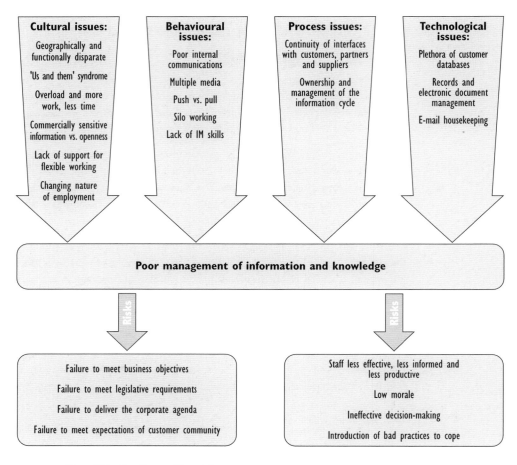

Figure 8.2 – Four facets of knowledge management

proper levels of support and enabling the processes of electronic document management? Does the technology enhance control and enable optimisation of the knowledge assets?

The illustration presents topics for you to consider. Consider also the risks inherent in failing to address knowledge management and information management. Knowledge management, or the failure to address knowledge management, will affect how you do business in terms of being efficient and agile. In the same way that you may decline to become involved about any of the topics in this book, you should do so only after a full and proper risk assessment of what you stand to lose if you fail to look after the most fundamental building block of the organisation – information.

8.4.1 Information management

The spectrum of records management through to knowledge management is often clouded with information management. This is not because information management is unimportant or less important but because the definitions or demarcation lines are diffuse or obscured. It is common to find information and knowledge management being used to describe the same things. Although a more rigorous definition of knowledge management would be the contextual definition of information assets, the definitions used simply need to be clear and clearly understood.

Information management in most organisations tends to be used in the records management arena; legislation means that managing public records is now a legal matter particularly in the area of data protection, privacy, freedom of information and disclosure.

Information management is, like knowledge management, a broad church and encompasses, *inter alia*, librarian skills (researching, indexing, cataloguing, storing and retrieval), electronic and paper management and cataloguing. Creation of organisational 'yellow pages' is often an information management project run under a knowledge programme.

Most important is the issue of ensuring that a policy exists to support whatever is the business directive being supported. As with standards, the creation of an appropriate policy for knowledge management or information management is more important than the method or standard itself. There are many ways to achieve business goals and setting policy is the key to proper selection of the tools.

Some organisations consider the issues to relate to information management, rather than knowledge management. The important thing is to recognise that each issue must be addressed corporately in order to achieve knowledge management goals that in turn facilitate other organisational issues discussed throughout this book.

For more information, Aslib (The Association for Information Management, www.aslib.co.uk) and ARMA (Association of Records Managers and Administrators, www.arma.org) are recommended.

Aslib publishes extensive training materials and publications about managing information assets while ARMA is a not-for-profit organisation with particular expertise in managing records (document and electronic) and extensive knowledge of compliance, risk and privacy issues. They were instrumental in the ISO Records Management Standard 15489.

8.5 Behavioural issues

8.5.1 Culture

The issue of cultural change has been mentioned throughout this chapter. Organisational culture is defined at Board level and cascades throughout. How you as an executive conduct your day-to-day business is the exemplar for your managers and for their staff. An open, sharing culture is possible only when it is demonstrated from the top. Allowing the silo mentality to be retained will signal failure for any knowledge management initiative (indeed any information management initiative too).

If you want a knowledge management initiative to succeed, be openly supportive of the initiative, demonstrate your support by adopting a sharing stance about all but sensitive information and make sure that knowledge management goals are attainable and demonstrable. And, as indicated above, emphasise collaboration as well as communication. Some personality types are more suitable for this task than others and such individuals who are openly collaborative should be sought out and used to mentor others.

8.5.2 Behaviour

In terms of behaviour, poor communications and (the result of poor communications) silo working, are the most obvious barriers to success. The toughest barrier to break down is nearly always the silo mentality, knowledge equating to power. Winning over sceptics can be done through persuasion, incentivisation and of course regulation. Inevitably, the regulatory response will cause friction and Human Resources (HR) policies will need to be in place that reward compliance with organisational policy and punish the recalcitrant.

No matter how successful you are at persuasion, someone somewhere will not wish to take part in change initiatives, or presume they are sufficiently special that corporate policy does not apply to them.

Poor communications will always be a problem in larger organisations, but for executive managers, the will to improve in this area should be sufficient to drive appropriate change. Being open and responsive and ensuring cascade of information as and when appropriate are obvious steps; less obvious is to regularly interrogate using surveys to ensure that what you perceive to be done is being enacted and well received.

Behavioural problems can also be caused by insufficient (and inappropriate) skills; in the knowledge management arena one of the principal skills is in document management, another in the broader area of information management. If information is not properly catalogued and filed it is not going to be retrievable in the most efficient way and will therefore militate against the embedding of knowledge management.

8.6 Knowledge management process

People, process and technology are the standard cornerstones in any major initiative. Culture, as already established, is a crucial element; people drive the definition of process, adoption of the process, implementation and continuous improvement. The theory around, for example, story telling as the key to knowledge management drives off the pragmatic. So what are the practical processes?

For a start, the processes of information management (identifying, tagging and cataloguing) must all be in place. There must be policies and processes to support information retrieval, use, reuse and disposal. Processes to audit information assets and identify (and close) gaps and processes to ensure compliance to regulatory matters (electronic records management, data protection and so on) must all be defined and policed.

8.6.1 Technology

Although knowledge management is not a technology issue, there is no doubt that technology can facilitate knowledge management. That does not mean that the *focus* should be on the technology, however. The technical questions that must be answered include:

- Is there an efficient intranet (indeed, is there an intranet)?
- Is the e-presence of the organisation coherent and properly linked to strategy?
- How many databases exist and how are they used?
- Is information properly organised in the databases and is it free from duplication?
- Are records management and electronic document management under proper control (for example, can you demonstrate compliance with standards)?
- Can you demonstrate policies for e-mail, e-mail housekeeping, data protection and public records housekeeping?

8.6.2 Case studies

A UK government example

To address the shortcomings identified in a UK government department, and to realise the potential benefits, a strategic vision for knowledge management was established: *to be the hub for the best knowledge on public procurement,* by stimulating the collection, development and deployment of the best knowledge of public procurement to ensure that government gets best value in its purchases of goods, services and capital projects.

Six objectives were set for knowledge management:

- raise awareness and gain widespread commitment to knowledge management and its contribution to departmental objectives
- systematically identify the best sources of knowledge in critical domains (such as customers, suppliers and procurement practice) and ensure that they are enhanced and exploited
- increase accessibility to the department's knowledge base by all who need it – staff, partners, customers and suppliers

- create and promote a culture where knowledge is naturally shared and where good knowledge management practices are embedded into everyday activities, so that knowledge is shared and learning is done before, during and after business activities
- create an organisational environment in which core knowledge management skills are enhanced
- ensure that an enabling technology framework is provided that meets the organisational needs for effective knowledge management.

The result of this was a process model that became the blueprint for pulling together the knowledge flows and directly led to creation of active communities that created, shared and cooperated in the exploitation of appropriate knowledge. Some were more successful than others. Those where the cultural issues that surround sharing were addressed by excellent leadership within the peer groups were very successful; those where a culture of 'knowledge is power' prevailed were less successful.

A visionary approach to IT was adopted, where the central tenet was one of sharing information and cross-referencing to facilitate sharing between former information silos was implemented. Only those willing to share were allowed to become part of the knowledge environment, an approach that soon led to awareness from those 'on the outside' that they were missing out! And IT systems were designed and specified to meet knowledge goals as well as business goals.

And what about the impact on ITSM? A business-centric Service Desk was created focused on knowledge-centred support (a concept endorsed by many organisations working in the Service Desk/helpdesk field, particularly in the USA), and ITIL was used to provide the guidance for identifying required processes, procedures and technology to equip the Service Desk. ITIL was also used to define change procedures, severity levels and all of the other aspects that ITSM experts see of value in ITIL.

Knowledge-centred support, ITSM and ITIL helped the newly created Service Desk to become effective in a remarkably short time, with the result that it became a flagship for both knowledge management and use of IT.

A private sector example

A leading multinational supplier of outsourcing embarked on an organisation-wide exercise to create a repository of policies. Central control over the policy-making activities was considered to be key to future efficiencies, and a project team was gathered to decide how this would be achieved.

The initial project scoping was predicated around knowledge management for the worldwide body, with the intranet being the embodiment of the knowledge repository and the creation of multiple teams to document all knowledge and to create a solution based on managing content. The premise was that all information would be recorded once only, properly meta-tagged and with the content systems driving the creation (through templates) of multiple views of the data, and with the ability to use the data electronically, on the Web, or to publish to varied media.

The reality of the scale of the project caused a major rethink, but not about the need to capture and reuse knowledge. If anything, the investigations around the knowledge assets of the organisation had caused even sceptics to realise the potential benefits of knowledge management. Rather, the rethinking was around the ability of the organisation to execute such an ambitious undertaking.

A cost-benefit analysis of the effect of proper management of knowledge assets was undertaken. Its mandate was that the project to be undertaken should realise major benefits through controlling the massive proliferation of information assets rather than through creation of an entirely different way of working. Such an approach would be intrinsically cheaper and easier to manage.

It was realised that even a very basic document management system, if installed and used correctly, would bring substantial knowledge management benefits simply by providing structure and accessibility.

IT personnel were used to assist the procurement process for required technology, but the business side led the creation of the requirement specification. The software that was acquired added significantly to the ability of the organisation to police areas of regulatory compliance too, because of the control of document creation and the ability to provide audit trails. Governance was a major issue for both the business and IT organisations, which had caused the project team to spend time thinking through the possible impact of the regulatory frameworks and identifying how strategic information assets could be managed to assist compliance.

8.6.3 Lessons to learn

There is an emerging consensus on the vision for knowledge and information within an organisation. It is one of *'Smarter Sharing'* – creating an environment where:

- sharing and collaboration is the norm, facilitated and enabled by IT
- the culture of the organisation recognises knowledge and information as a key asset, needing to be managed and fully exploited, and capable of generating significant returns
- the organisation rejects the 'knowledge is power' philosophy
- staff are equipped to act as ambassadors for the organisation
- information is collected and stored only once, wherever possible
- information assets that are under control in a knowledge management environment contribute to regulatory compliance as well as to organisational efficiency

- information is stored and managed flexibly so that it can be linked, processed and properly maintained, and presented for different audiences

- the ethos is for information to be open and accessible, but with recognition of the need to manage this within the constraints of commercially sensitive information

- the infrastructure, tools and processes required to support knowledge and information management are appropriate and continually developed to avoid stagnation.

8.6.4 Achieving the vision

Achieving the vision will require change – changes in behaviour, attitudes, skills, competencies and culture – and of course will need to be well-policed and have appropriate processes and policies. Support and buy-in from executive Board members as well as from individuals throughout the organisation is an absolute requirement.

Ideally, there should be a body to provide a 'steer' for achieving the vision, to agree priorities and how resources will be created and supported, and to define visionary approaches to IT, creating systems to support new ways of working, facilitating sharing, etc., all within an appropriate IT infrastructure.

There must also be a programme of work and the resources to support it.

All these requirements point to a need for a framework for enabling organisations to better manage their knowledge and information. However, the framework needs to take account of the overall business strategy as well as the problems and issues that already exist and need to be addressed.

Finally, HR policies that incentivise knowledge sharing and discourage 'knowledge is power' should be created and implemented. Many organisations have discovered that this one key message is a huge step in making knowledge management initiatives succeed.

8.6.5 Quick checklists

Asking the right questions

- How critical is information to the organisation and how critical is the timely availability of the information?

- How far should the organisation go in its investment in knowledge management and are the benefits commensurate with the cost?

- Is knowledge management a regular item on the agenda for Board discussion?

- Is the reporting level of the most senior knowledge management manager commensurate with the importance of knowledge?

- Does the Board ask questions about managing its information?

- Does the Board approve the knowledge management strategy and for the information management strategy?
- Is IT delivering the technology to support knowledge management?
- Is knowledge management a business issue?

IT issues

- Is knowledge management dependent on IT?
- Does IT management meet with business management to develop strategies for knowledge management, information management and document management?
- Does the organisation's records manager meet regularly with IT managers?
- Who holds the budgets for the technology required to meet records management requirements?
- Is IT governance management linked to the knowledge management strategy to ensure auditability?
- How is business continuity planning supported by the technology underpinning the knowledge management systems?
- Does IT support knowledge communities?
- Are the information assets regularly scrutinised for applicability, potential and accuracy?

Key points

- Maintain a summarised background of knowledge management in the organisation.
- Maintain a summarised background of information management in the organisation.
- Appoint an organisational records manager.
- Know where knowledge management and information management fit in the wider context of the organisation.
- Maintain a simple framework to help people think about the issues:
  - value
  - strategic alignment
  - risks of failing to manage key assets
  - metrics that will illustrate benefit and that can be understood at Board level.
- Ask probing questions.
- Identify critical success factors.
- Benchmark the organisation against others.

9 STANDARDS AND BEST PRACTICE

9.1 Key messages for the Board

Standards and best practice are important. They can provide the basis for a framework of IT governance that demonstrates proof of good management practices in use. They can be used as a goal for quality improvements to aim for. Standards and best practice provide the basis for a common approach by many different organisations, including a supply chain of suppliers, lead suppliers and subcontracted suppliers. A common approach from adoption of standards and best practice also reduces costs as automation becomes easier and cheaper. There will be improved interoperability of tools. Proof that an organisation has achieved an agreed level of good practice can give managers confidence that products and services will be delivered to an agreed and verifiable quality.

9.2 Introduction

The variety of standards and best practice approaches presents management with a dilemma, especially as many represent a long-term financial commitment. As a manager, which do I use?

There are *standards*, which have been formally defined, such as ISO standards, and adopted as international or national standards. There are also other components that make up a framework of good practice for an organisation's internal procedures to manage its IT services. There may be widely used approaches such as ITIL or CobiT. While these are not formal standards, they are important because they enable the organisation to develop its own internal standards of good practice.

Selection of the best match for any one organisation should be directly linked to business drivers, usually represented as policies, representing management direction.

Using a house-building analogy, if one driver is to reduce costs and pollution, the use of solar power becomes a policy. To use solar power you will need quality criteria for selection, testing, acceptance and installation – and if living in the UK, a contingency plan.

Organisations need the IT department or IT service provider to have internal policies to give management direction on, *inter alia*, legislation, governance, quality, programme and project planning and management of the IT domain. There are many options for this, many supporting the same domain. Just two examples are PRINCE2 and PMI methods which both apply to project management. It is not possible to provide a definitive mapping of every example as they cover a wide variety of differences in objectives, scope and approach.

It is misleading to advise that any one example will be suitable, as no all-embracing, fully supported example exists. Figure 9.1 represents only some of the better known examples and is not intended to be used to support decision-making.

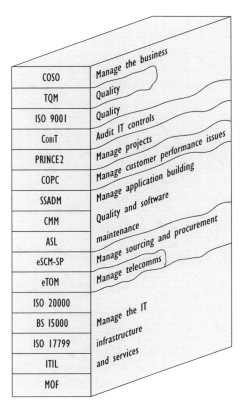

Figure 9.1 – Example standards and best practice approaches

9.3 Why the confusion?

In the example in Section 9.2, if a particular set of *standards and best practice approaches* is considered suitable for supporting policies, this assumption must be tested. This involves identifying the touch-points, constraints, overlaps or conflicts. This is not normally a simple task and sufficient time must be allowed for this to be done properly. Although standards and best practice change over time, the changes are part of a managed process as a balance is struck between the inclusion of the latest good practice, the benefits these will bring and the cost of managing the changes, such as staff retraining or tool amendments. It is something of a myth that best practice will be constantly updated; a more accurate description is phased improvements.

An organisation's business drivers do change and may change rapidly and unexpectedly. The changes may not be under the direct control of the organisation. Changes to drivers may result from legislation, regulations, business operating environment or financial pressures. This range of changes must be catered for by adapting or replacing the set of selected standards and best practice approaches. This adaptability should be considered when selecting those to be used. The more options that are being used to support policies the more complex the management overhead becomes. Often, a conflict will arise with selection as each option being considered may have avid and determined supporters, who may have obtained qualifications or experience with their favoured candidate.

9.4 Competing pressures

Before reviewing the various options to determine which one is 'the best' the question that must be asked is '*Why* is this standard, model, method or framework required?' Is it because of development work that is late, of poor quality or over budget? Is it because availability requirements are not met? Is it because the cost of IT services means they are not value for money to the customer's business? Or is it because the organisation must comply with specific legislation or regulations? Often the CEO or the Board wishes compliance to be based on a particular reference model because of legislative or market drivers. This is common where a sector has developed a consensus on 'the best'. This normally means the management of IT services is directed to adopt this option and to ensure compliance is achieved by the IT department.

Once a 'best fit' option is chosen it is important to also understand how changes to the IT and operating environment will be accommodated. Changes may be a result of many things – different business requirements or new technology. Changes (and potential changes) need to be monitored or they will undermine the selected option so that policies are not supported and business drivers are not achieved.

One well-publicised example is the Sarbanes-Oxley Act, under which US companies (or those companies that trade with the US) must be able to demonstrate that adequate internal controls have been used to safeguard confidential information from being compromised. Failure to comply with this act has serious repercussions for both companies and their senior management, as individuals.

Even the right 'best fit' option can fail. This is usually distraction that causes delays and rework during implementation, and even project closure.

To summarise, the steps to determine which option (or options) would be best for your organisation are as follows:

- select and create policies that support the business drivers
- agree what difficulty is to be resolved

- agree the business drivers that are to be addressed

- review the available options – do not be limited to only one. Unless a very specific goal is being addressed (say, controlling the Incident Management process, where ITIL would be one of the key candidates), it is unlikely that a single option will be adequate

- ensure that it is understood how each option under consideration is used

- evaluate against the business drivers and policies

- define the measurements that will result from or support each option

- map the scope, interfaces, inputs and outputs for each option to avoid 'competing' options causing conflict between groups wrestling for control of one or more options, rather than working to deliver against the organisation's business drivers.

Decision-making can be assisted by agreeing what to measure, which in turn is influenced by what is to be achieved. Is the intention to outsource? Is radical change being managed? Is the driver the legislative requirements? These questions must be answered to arrive at a set of measures used to ensure that the options selected are appropriate. For example, why select a structured systems design method but then not measure its effectiveness?

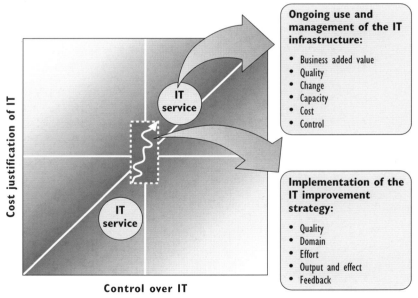

Figure 9.2 – What to measure?

9.5 Defining internal policies for managing IT services

Differences in available standards and best practice approaches are mainly in the scope and depth of detail. Best practice approaches such as ITIL are relatively easy to use because ITIL is largely 'what to do' rather than a 'how to…'.

Many of the 'how to' models are proprietary. Some examples, as illustrations *not* recommendations, include the HP ITSM reference model, CA's EIM/EDM, or the HDI Service Support models. Many proprietary models are used by the owner when installing their own software or providing services to assist embedding non-proprietary methods and models. As long as the business drivers and policies are supported the selection can be a mix of proprietary and non-proprietary reference models.

Be cautious about what can (and cannot) be achieved by use of an individual option. For example, it is a common misconception that implementing the CobiT model guarantees compliance with US Sarbanes-Oxley legislation. Even a good option can be used badly. Complying with Sarbanes-Oxley legislation is far more complex than simply implementation of an option (or even a number of options). Audit organisations often cite that individual auditors differ in their approach to assignments, within the limits set by each audit scheme. Neither does reliance on IT software guarantee compliance. Again, it is important to stress the needs of the organisation's business drivers informing policies, which in turn are supported by the best fit options, which require clarity on what is to be achieved and how it can be measured.

9.6 Roles

Figure 9.3 illustrates another aspect of the selection process. You must decide what roles are needed. Many of the roles will map to a single option (or policy). All of those shown in Figure 9.3 are normally required. Using a non-IT example, in building a house the role of architect is necessary, and also the roles of suppliers, builders, financial control, quality control and many others, each contributing to the ultimate goal of building the house required. Not all roles will be filled by separate individuals. One person may have several roles. Some roles should not be combined. For example, when building a house you would want quality checks on electricity installation done by someone other than the person who did the installation.

The focus on achieving a pre-defined goal is central to Figure 9.4, ensuring that business drivers, internal policies for managing IT services and service goals are in harmony. The fulfilment of business drivers must always be the most important principle, overriding the IT provider's view about whether 'model x' or 'method y' is best. Too often a model or method is superficially beguiling but may not bring real value.

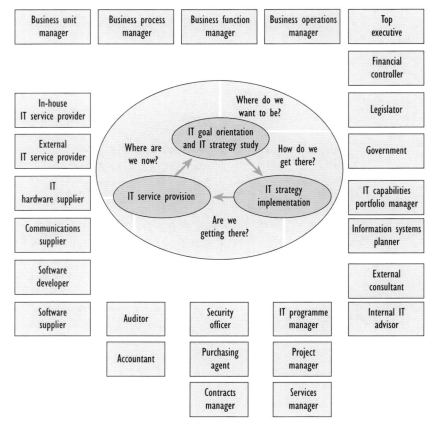

Figure 9.3 – Roles

9.7 Business model for adopting ITIL

Of course, this is an ITIL volume and therefore requires a description of a business model that can be used simply and flexibly to justify the adoption of ITIL. The illustration in this section is included to help identify the business drivers, policies and measures that must be supported. The illustration should be used to drive three principal outcomes:

- define business needs for IT with a view to resolving any misalignment between the business and IT while avoiding unrealistic or impractical expectations about use of IT on the part of the business

- define requirements for IT capabilities with a view to meeting the business needs for IT and achieving optimal deployment of IT in the business

- align needs and goals of the business with the IT infrastructure, its IT capabilities and opportunities in the market.

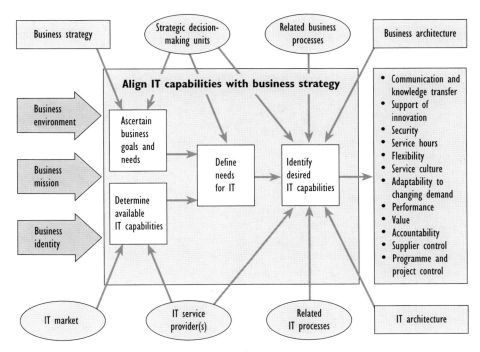

Figure 9.4 – Principal outcomes of implementing a framework of good practice

9.8 Putting the pieces together

Options exist for all the topics in Figure 9.4. This section discusses how to combine the most appropriate options to support an organisation's business drivers.

Consider an organisation that has used ITIL to implement best practice processes and procedures and now wishes to achieve a demonstrable programme of measurements leading to certification against a standard.

For an organisation to fully realise ITSM capability, it must embrace not only the key aspects necessary to build ITSM capability but also those required to improve capability. Figure 9.5 shows how ISO/IEC 20000 and the Capability Maturity Model (CMM) drive ITSM enablers and measurements, and measurements drive enablers.

Organisations tend to focus on too narrow a scope for improving their capabilities. This results in limited and low-quality processes and services, adding too little value.

A key success factor is that process:process measurement and standards must be *instituted in tandem* to realise and continually improve capability. The approach in Figure 9.6 is a more productive approach to adopt.

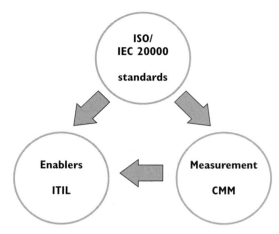

Figure 9.5 – The component pieces

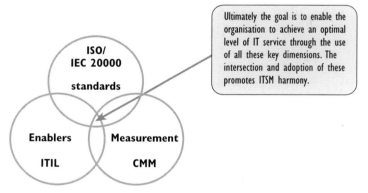

Figure 9.6 – Integration

The range of 'best practices' that can be used is enormous. It is not the intention of an ITIL volume to provide a definitive compendium, or to describe all possible permutations of use.

10 BIBLIOGRAPHY AND FURTHER INFORMATION

10.1 OGC publications

Application Management
OGC, 2002
Available from TSO, www.tso.co.uk
ISBN 0-11-330866-3

Business Perspective: The IS View on Delivering Services to the Business
OGC, 2002
Available from TSO, www.tso.co.uk
ISBN 0-11-330894-9

ICT Infrastructure Management
OGC, 2002
Available from TSO, www.tso.co.uk
ISBN 0-11-330865-5

Management of Risk
OGC, 2005
Available from TSO, www.tso.co.uk
ISBN 0-11-330909-0

Managing Successful Programmes
OGC, 2005
Available from TSO, www.tso.co.uk
ISBN 0-11-330917-1

Managing Successful Projects with PRINCE2
OGC, 2005
Available from TSO, www.tso.co.uk
ISBN 0-11-330946-5

Planning to Implement Service Management
OGC, 2005
Available from TSO, www.tso.co.uk
ISBN 0-11-330877-9

Security Management
OGC, 2004
Available from TSO, www.tso.co.uk
ISBN 0-11-330014-X

Service Delivery
OGC, 2001
Available from TSO, www.tso.co.uk
ISBN 0-11-330017-4

Service Support
OGC, 2000
Available from TSO, www.tso.co.uk
ISBN 0-11-330015-8

Software Asset Management
OGC, 2003
Available from TSO, www.tso.co.uk
ISBN 0-11-330943-0

OGC *IT Supplier Code of Best Practice*, Intellect 2003
www.ogc.gov.uk/embedded_object.asp?docid=1004859

Successful Delivery Toolkit, available on the OGC website
www.ogc.gov.uk

The official ITIL website
www.itil.co.uk

10.2   Other publications and information sources

IT governance resources

IT Governance – How Top Performers Manage IT Decision Rights for Superior Results
Weill, Peter and Ross, Jeanne, 2004
Harvard Business School Press
ISBN 1-59139-253-5
This book documents the research into best practice IT governance from the MIT
Sloan School of Management Center for Information Systems Research (CISR).

The Balanced Scorecard: Translating Strategy into Action
Kaplan, R.S. and Norton, D.P., 1996
Harvard Business School Press
ISBN 0875846513

The Fifth Discipline – The Art & Practice of the Learning Organisation
Senge, Peter, 1994
Century Business
ISBN 0385260954

Background on corporate governance from the Institute of Governance
www.iog.ca

IT Governance Institute and CobiT
www.itgovernance.org
www.isaca.org/cobit.htm
These Internet sites provide an important resource for IS assurance, control, security and
IT governance best practice.

Change Management resources

Managing Change And Transition
Harvard Business Essentials, 2003
Harvard Business School Press, Boston, Massachusetts, USA

On Leading Change
Hesselbein, Frances and Johnston, Rob, 2002
Jossey-Bass, San Francisco, California, USA

The Orange Book – Management Of Risk – Principles And Concepts
HM Treasury, Crown Copyright, UK, 2004

Winning at Change
Kotter, John P.
Leader to Leader No. 10, Fall 1998
Leader to Leader Institute
http://leadertoleader.org/leaderbooks/L2L/fall98/kotter.html

Canadian Organisational Behavior
McShane, Steven L., 2001
McGraw-Hill Ryerson, Toronto, Ontario, Canada

Organizational Behavior
Osland, Joyce S., Kolb, David A. and Rubin, Irwin M., 2001
Prentice Hall, Upper Saddle River, New Jersey, USA

Managing Change At Work
Scott, Cynthia D. and Jaffe, Dennis T., 1989
Crisp Publications, Canada

Business continuity resources

When IT lifts productivity
The McKinsey Quarterly, 2004 no. 4

AMR Research
www.amr-research.com

Basel Committee for Banking Supervision
www.bis.org/bcbs

Boston Consulting Group
www.bcg.com

Business Continuity Institute
www.thebci.org

Butler Group
www.butlergroup.com

Institute of Chartered Accountants – Centre for Business Performance
www.icaew.co.uk/index.afm?route=127752

Ontrack Data International
www.ontrack.com

Survive
www.survive.com

The Uptime Institute
www.uptimeinstitute.com

IT asset management resources

Management Update: IT Asset Management is Mandatory, Not Optional
O'Brien, F., 20 August 2003
Article ref. IGG-08202003-01

Why IT Asset Management is Important Now
O'Brien, F., 10 June 2004
Article Ref: AV-23-0633

First Annual BSA and IDC Global Software Piracy Study
BSA/IDC July 2004

Sourcing resources

Outsourcing: A CIO's Perspective
Williams, Oakie, 1 June 1998
CRC Press
ISBN 1574442163

Definitive List of Outsourcing Books
http://attitudeweb.be/resources/books/outsourcing/index_en.php?page=1

Offshore Outsourcing Information Centre
www.rttsweb.com/services/outsourcing/info_center.cfm

e-Sourcing Capabilities Model for Service Providers (eSCM-SP) Version 2.0
http://itsqc.cs.cmu.edu

Knowledge management resources

Knowledge Management Review
Gulas, Victor
Montgomery Watson Harza
Vol 5 Issue 3, www.melcrum.com

The Help Desk Institute publishes a book on their application of ITIL within the
context of Knowledge Centered Support (KCS), *Implementing Service and Support
Management Processes: A Practical Guide*, 2005, www.thinkhdi.com

KM forum
www.km-forum.org

KM world
www.kmworld.com

The Knowledge Management Resource Center
www.kmresource.com

For more information about information management, Aslib (The Association for
Information Management www.aslib.co.uk) and ARMA (Association of Records
Managers and Administrators www.arma.org) are recommended.

Standards and best practice resources

HP ITSM reference model
http://h20219.www2.hp.com/services/cache/78360-0-0-225-121.html

CA's EIM/EDM
http://ca.com

HDI Service Support models
www.thinkhdi.com

ISO/IEC 20000

www.iso.org

www.bsi-global.com

www.itSMF.com

Risk management resources

The APM Group provides accreditation for the OGC's Management of Risk qualifications and can be accessed through
www.m-o-r.org/web/site/home/home.asp

Further details on Basel II can be found through the Bank for International Settlements (BIS) website
www.bis.org/publ/bcbsca.htm

Corporate Governance reports and guidance from around the world, and including the UK's Turnbull, Combined Code, Hampel, Greenbury and Cadbury documentation can be found via the European Corporate Governance Institute (ECGI) at
www.ecgi.org/codes/all_codes.php

Details regarding the FSA's Integrated Prudential Sourcebook (PSB) can be found at
www.fsa.gov.uk

Global Association of Risk Professionals
www.garp.com

The Institute of Risk Management
www.theirm.org

The National Forum for Risk Management in the Public Sector
www.alarm-uk.com

Operational Risk Research Forum
www.orrf.org (including the Institute of Operational Risk)

The Sarbanes-Oxley reference website can be accessed at
www.sarbanes-oxley.com

Quality Management resources

www.deming.org

www.efqm.org

www.quality.nist.gov

Appendix A LIST OF ACRONYMS AND GLOSSARY

A.1 Acronyms

CAB	Change Advisory Board
CI	Configuration Item
CMDB	Configuration Management Database
CobiT	Control Objectives for Information and related Technology
CSF	Critical success factor
EFQM	European Foundation for Quality Management
FM	Facilities management
ISO	International Organization for Standardization
IT	Information technology
ITAM	IT asset management
ITIL	IT Infrastructure Library
ITSM	IT Service Management
itSMF	IT Service Management Forum
KPI	Key performance indicator
OGC	Office of Government Commerce
PIR	Post implementation review
QMS	Quality Management System
SLA	Service Level Agreement
TQM	Total Quality Management

A.2   Glossary

Asset

Something that contributes to an IT service. Assets can include people, accommodation, servers, software, data, networks, paper records, telephones, etc.

Assets that need to be individually managed are also Configuration Items. For example, the door lock on a computer room or a consumable item would not be a Configuration Item.

In the context of financial management, items below a specific value are not considered to be assets as it would not be cost-effective to track and manage them.

Backup

Copying data to protect against loss of integrity or availability of the original.

Balanced Scorecard

A management tool developed by Drs Robert Kaplan (Harvard Business School) and David Norton. A Balanced Scorecard enables a strategy to be broken down into key performance indicators (KPIs). Performance against the KPIs is used to demonstrate how well the strategy is being achieved. A Balanced Scorecard has four major areas, each of which has a small number of KPIs. The same four areas are considered at different levels of detail throughout the organisation.

British Standards Institution (BSI)

The UK National Standards body, responsible for creating and maintaining British Standards. See www.bsi-global.com for more information.

Change

The addition, modification or removal of anything that could have an effect on IT services. The scope should include all Configuration Items, processes, documentation etc.

Change Advisory Board (CAB)

A group of people that assists the Change Manager in the assessment, prioritisation and scheduling of changes. This board is usually made up of representatives from all areas within the IT service provider, representatives from the business, and third parties such as suppliers.

Change Management

The process responsible for controlling the lifecycle of all changes. The primary objective of Change Management is to enable beneficial changes to be made, with minimum disruption to IT services.

CobiT

Control Objectives for Information and related Technology (CobiT) provides guidance and best practice for the management of IT processes. CobiT is published by the IT Governance Institute. See www.isaca.org for more information.

Configuration Item (CI)

Any component that needs to be managed in order to deliver an IT service. Information about each CI is recorded in a configuration record within the CMDB and is maintained throughout its lifecycle by Configuration Management. CIs are under the control of Change Management. CIs typically include hardware, software, buildings, people, and formal documentation such as process documentation and SLAs.

Configuration Management

The process responsible for maintaining information about Configuration Items required to deliver an IT service, including their relationships. This information is managed throughout the lifecycle of the CI. The primary objective of Configuration Management is to underpin the delivery of IT services by providing accurate data to all IT Service Management processes when and where it is needed.

Configuration Management Database (CMDB)

A database used to manage Configuration Records throughout their lifecycle. The CMDB records the attributes of each CI, and relationships with other CIs. A CMDB may also contain other information linked to CIs, for example incident, problem or change records. The CMDB is maintained by Configuration Management and is used by all IT Service Management processes.

Contracting out

The process of buying in services, which were previously provided in-house, from a third party. In IT terms it encompasses concepts such as facilities management, outsourcing, turnkeys, etc. Also known as *outsourcing*.

Control

A means of managing a risk, or ensuring that a business objective is achieved. Example controls include policies, procedures, roles, software configurations, passwords, RAID, fences, door locks, etc. A control is sometimes called a countermeasure or safeguard. Control is also used as a generic term to manage something.

Control Objectives for Information and related Technology (CobiT)

See CobiT.

Corporate governance

The process by which the Board carries out and discharges its accountabilities and responsibilities (legal, moral and regulatory).

Corporate risk

Risks specific to the organisation's corporate responsibilities.

Critical success factor (CSF)

Something that must happen if a process, project, plan or IT service is to succeed. KPIs are used to measure the achievement of each CSF. For example, a CSF of 'protect IT services when making changes' could be measured by KPIs such as 'percentage reduction of unsuccessful changes', 'percentage reduction in changes causing incidents', etc.

Customer

Used in this book to mean an entire organisation (including the business and IT directorate) which is involved in relationships with one or more suppliers, usually involving purchases of products and services.

Distributed computing

Where a large problem is solved by splitting the problem between many computers to solve and then combining the solution.

End-user

Any person using an IT service.

European Foundation for Quality Management

The EFQM Excellence Model was introduced at the beginning of 1992 as the framework for assessing organisations for the European Quality Award. It is now the most widely used organisational framework in Europe and it has become the basis for the majority of national and regional Quality Awards. See www.efqm.org for more information.

Exposure

The vulnerability to a particular risk and susceptibility to loss.

Facilities management (FM)

The provision of the management, operation and support of an organisation's IT services and IT infrastructure activities by an external source at agreed service levels. The services are generally provided for a set time at an agreed cost.

Incident

An unplanned interruption to an IT service or reduction in the quality of an IT service. Any event which could affect an IT service in the future is also an incident. For example, failure of one disk from a mirror set.

Incident Management

The process responsible for managing the lifecycle of all incidents. The primary objective of Incident Management is to return the IT service to customers as quickly as possible.

Information technology (IT)

The use of technology for the storage, communication or processing of information. The technology typically includes computers, telecommunications, applications and other software. The information may include business data, voice, images, video, etc. Information technology is often used to support business processes through IT services.

Informed Customer

A manager who works for the customer, and is a specialist in dealing with and managing IT service providers. The Informed Customer is responsible for all aspects of managing the relationship with service providers.

Inherent risk

The possibility that an incident will have an adverse impact on the assets of an organisation which cannot be managed or transferred.

Internal control

The tangible and intangible means that can be employed to ensure business objectives are met.

International Organization for Standardization (ISO)

The International Organization for Standardization (ISO) is the world's largest developer of standards. ISO is a non-governmental organisation which is a network of the national standards institutes of 156 countries. Further information about ISO is available from www.iso.org.

IT department/directorate

That part of an organisation which has responsibility for IT strategy and standards, and controls the development and provision of IT systems and services for the organisation.

IT Infrastructure Library (ITIL)

A set of best practice guidance for IT Service Management. ITIL is owned by the OGC and is developed in conjunction with the *it*SMF. ITIL consists of a series of publications giving guidance on the provision of quality IT services, and on the processes and facilities needed to support them. See www.ogc.gov.uk/index.asp?id=2261 for more information.

IT Service Management (ITSM)

The implementation and management of quality IT services that meet the needs of the business. IT Service Management is performed by IT service providers through an appropriate mix of people, process and information technology.

IT Service Management Forum (*it*SMF)

The IT Service Management Forum is an independent organisation dedicated to promoting a professional approach to IT Service Management. The *it*SMF is a not-for-profit membership organisation with representation in many countries around the world (*it*SMF Chapters). The *it*SMF and its membership contribute to the development of ITIL and associated IT Service Management Standards. See www.itsmf.com for more information.

IT Service Manager

The person with overall responsibility for IT service quality. Typically his/her peers are the Applications Development Manager and the Administration and Finance Manager, and all report to the organisation's Director of IT.

IT service provider

A service provider that provides IT services to internal customers or external customers.

IT services

That part of the IT department/directorate which is responsible for providing and managing IT services to support one or more business areas within an organisation.

Key performance indicator (KPI)

A metric that is used to help manage a process, IT service or activity. Many metrics may be measured, but only the most important of these are defined as KPIs and used to actively manage and report on the process, IT service or activity. KPIs should be selected to ensure that efficiency, effectiveness, and cost-effectiveness are all managed. See Critical success factor.

Lifecycle

The various stages in the life of a Configuration Item, incident, problem, change etc. The lifecycle defines the categories for status and the status transitions that are permitted. For example:

The lifecycle of an application includes design, build, test, deploy, operate etc.

The lifecycle of an incident includes detect, respond, diagnose, repair, recover, restore.

The lifecycle of a server may include: ordered, received, in test, live, disposed etc.

Management of risk (M_o_R)

OGC's recommended approach for managing risk.

Managing Successful Programmes (MSP)

OGC's recommended approach for managing programmes of change.

Mission-critical activities

> The critical operational activities without which the organisation will quickly be unable to achieve its business objectives.

Mitigation

> An activity or process which will counter the risk or the impact of the risk.

Office of Government Commerce (OGC)

> OGC owns the copyright to the ITIL publications. It is a UK government department that works with public sector organisations to help them improve their efficiency, gain better value for money from their commercial activities, and deliver improved success from programmes and projects.

Operational risk

> The risk that deficiency in information services or internal controls will result in unexpected loss. These are normally associated with human error, system failure and inadequate process and control.

Outage

> The period of time that a service is expected to be unavailable and has a detrimental impact on the business.

Outsourcing

> Work being completed by a service provider outside the organisation. See Contracting out.

Plan-Do-Check-Act

> A four-stage cycle for Process Management, devised by Edward Deming. Plan-Do-Check-Act is also called the Deming Cycle.
>
> PLAN: Design or revise processes that support the IT services.
>
> DO: Implement the plan and manage the processes.
>
> CHECK: Measure the processes and IT services, compare with objectives and produce reports.
>
> ACT: Plan and implement changes to improve the processes.

Portfolio management

> Portfolio management is a centralised function that records, tracks and knows the business justification for and the interrelation between programmes and projects and their utilisation of resources organisation-wide.

Post implementation review (PIR)

> A review that takes place after a change or a project has been implemented. A PIR determines if the change or project was successful, and identifies opportunities for improvement.

PRINCE2 (PRojects IN a Controlled Environment)

The standard UK government methodology for project management.

Programme management

Programme management is the umbrella under which a number of projects are managed and monitored. Programme management oversees the related projects from start to finish, seeing the transformation through to its completion. See also OGC's Managing Successful Programmes, which is widely adopted as a standards-based approach to managing change programmes.

Project management

Project management is the process that enables project teams to coordinate their efforts in order to meet their objectives and goals. Ensuring that the right product or service is delivered at the right time, for the right customer, within the parameters of people, budget and time. See also OGC's PRINCE2 *(PRojects IN a Controlled Environment)*, which is widely adopted as a standards-based approach to managing projects.

Quality Management System (QMS)

The set of processes responsible for ensuring that all work carried out by an organisation is of a suitable quality to reliably meet business objectives or service levels.

Recovery

Returning a Configuration Item or an IT service to a working state. Recovery of an IT service often includes recovering data to a known consistent state. After recovery, further steps may be needed before the IT service can be made available to the users (restoration).

Release Management

The process responsible for planning, scheduling and controlling the movement of releases to test and live environments. The primary objective of Release Management is to ensure that the integrity of the live environment is protected and that the correct components are released. Release Management works closely with Configuration Management and Change Management.

Return on investment (ROI)

A measurement of the expected benefit of an investment. Calculated by dividing the average increase in financial benefit (taken over an agreed number of years) by the investment.

Restore

Taking action to return an IT service to the users after repair and recovery from an incident. This is the primary objective of Incident Management.

Risk

The possibility of suffering harm or loss. In quantitative risk management this is calculated as how likely it is that a specific threat will exploit a particular vulnerability.

Risk management

The process responsible for identifying, assessing and managing risks. Risk management can be quantitative (based on numerical data) or qualitative.

Rollout

Synonym for deployment. Most often used to refer to complex or phased deployments.

Scenario

A defined set of business and service conditions that can be used to test the service continuity plan.

Service continuity plan

A clearly defined and documented plan to address a service continuity event covering the personnel, resources, activities and services required to manage the event.

Service Desk

The single point of contact between the service provider and the users. A typical Service Desk manages incidents and service requests, and also handles communication with the users.

Service level

Measured and reported achievement against one or more Service Level Targets. Service level is sometimes used as an informal term to mean Service Level Target.

Service Level Agreement (SLA)

An agreement between an IT service provider and a customer. The SLA describes the IT service, documents Service Level Targets, and specifies the responsibilities of the IT service provider and the customer. A single SLA may cover multiple IT services or multiple customers.

Service Level Management (SLM)

The process responsible for negotiating Service Level Agreements, and ensuring that these are met. SLM is responsible for ensuring that all IT Service Management processes, Operational Level Agreements, and Underpinning Contracts are appropriate for the agreed Service Level Targets. SLM monitors and reports on service levels, and holds regular customer reviews.

Service provider

An organisation supplying services to one or more customers. Service provider is often used as an abbreviation for IT service provider.

Service Support

The core IT Service Management processes that have an operational focus. These are Incident Management, Problem Management, Configuration Management, Change Management and Release Management. Service Support also includes the Service Desk.

Supplier

Any organisation, external to the customer organisation, currently supplying, or with the potential to supply, products or services to a customer with or without a formal contract. See also service provider.

Systemic risk

A risk arising from a component failure which has a knock-on impact or upon which mission-critical activities rely.

Total Quality Management (TQM)

A methodology for managing continuous improvement by using a Quality Management System. TQM establishes a culture involving all people in the organisation in a process of continuous monitoring and improvement.

Unexpected loss

The worst-case financial loss that could arise from a service continuity event, calculated as the anticipated loss times the volatility of this value.

Appendix B ITIL

B.1 Introduction

ITIL, developed and owned by OGC, provides a framework of best practice guidance for IT Service Management. It is the most widely used and accepted approach to IT Service Management in the world.

The challenges for IT managers are to coordinate and work in partnership with the business to deliver high quality services. This has to be achieved while reducing the overall total cost of ownership and often increasing the frequency, complexity and volume of change. IT management is all about the efficient and effective use of the four Ps: people, processes, products (tools and technology) and partners (suppliers, vendors and outsourcing organisations). The people and process aspects must be addressed first; this is one of the core principles of ITIL. Another core principle is quality customer service.

ITIL provides 'best practice' guidelines and architectures to ensure that IT processes are closely aligned to business processes and that IT delivers the correct and appropriate business solutions. ITIL is not a set of rules or regulations and therefore tools, processes and people cannot be deemed 'ITIL compliant'. Processes and service providers can be assessed against ISO/IEC 20000-1, Information technology – Service management – Part 1: Specification.

This appendix outlines the ITIL framework.

B.2 The ITIL framework

ITIL provides comprehensive 'best practice' guidelines on all aspects of 'end-to-end' Service Management and covers the complete spectrum of people, processes, products and the use of partners. ITIL was initially designed and developed in the 1980s by UK government but has recently been revised and updated by OGC to bring it in line with modern practices, distributed computing and the Internet. ITIL is the most widely used management approach to the delivery and support of IT services and infrastructure, worldwide. ITIL and its constituent modules were scoped and developed within an overall framework.

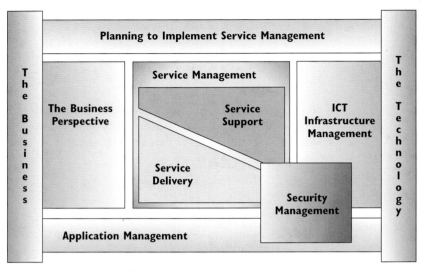

Figure B.1 – The ITIL framework

Figure B.1 shows the overall environment and structure within which the modules were produced. It illustrates the relationship that each of the modules has with the business and the technology. From the diagram it can be seen how The Business Perspective module is more closely aligned to the business and the ICT Infrastructure Management module is more closely aligned with the technology itself. The Service Delivery and Service Support modules provide the heart of the process framework.

These seven modules constitute the core of ITIL. Its recent revision has improved the structure of ITIL, and the new scope, contents and relationships of the various modules are in essence as follows.

Service Delivery: covers the processes required for the planning and delivery of quality IT services and looks at the longer-term processes associated with improving the quality of IT services delivered.

Service Support: describes the processes associated with the day-to-day support and maintenance activities associated with the provision of IT services.

ICT Infrastructure Management (ICT IM): covers all aspects of ICT Infrastructure Management from identification of business requirements through the tendering process, to the testing, installation, deployment, and ongoing operation and optimisation of the ICT components and IT services.

Planning to Implement Service Management: examines the issues and tasks involved in planning, implementing and improving Service Management processes within an organisation. It also addresses the issues associated with addressing cultural and organisational change, the development of a vision and strategy and the most appropriate method of approach.

Application Management: describes how to manage applications from the initial business need, through all stages in the application lifecycle, up to and including retirement. It places emphasis on ensuring that IT projects and strategies are tightly aligned with those of the business throughout the application lifecycle, to ensure that the business obtains best value from its investment.

The Business Perspective 1: provides advice and guidance to help IT personnel to understand how they can contribute to the business objectives and how their roles and services can be better aligned and exploited to maximise that contribution.

Security Management: details the process of planning and managing a defined level of security for information and IT services, including all aspects associated with reaction to security incidents. It also includes the assessment and management of risks and vulnerabilities, and the implementation of cost justifiable countermeasures.

B.3   Deliverables and interfaces

Figure B.2 illustrates the scope of each of the core ITIL modules together with the main deliverables from each of the individual processes, as shown within each of the individual process boxes. The lines between processes indicate where the deliverables of each process are principally used outside of their own process area.

B.4   Related standards and complementary guidance

ITIL consists of modules containing advice and guidance on 'best practice' relating to the provision of IT services. ITIL and ISO/IEC 20000 are aligned, as described in Appendix D.

A managers' guide to service management (BIP 0005) is intended for managers who are new to support services or who are faced with major changes to their existing support facility. This book takes the form of informative explanations, guidance and recommendations and acts as an introduction to ITIL.

IT service management – self-assessment workbook (PD 0015) is an easy to use checklist that complements ISO/IEC 20000 and is designed to assist an organisation's internal assessment of their services and the extent to which they conform to the specified requirements in ISO/IEC 20000.

The 'Achieving ISO/IEC 20000' series

Management decisions and documentation (BIP 0030)

Why people matter (BIP 0031)

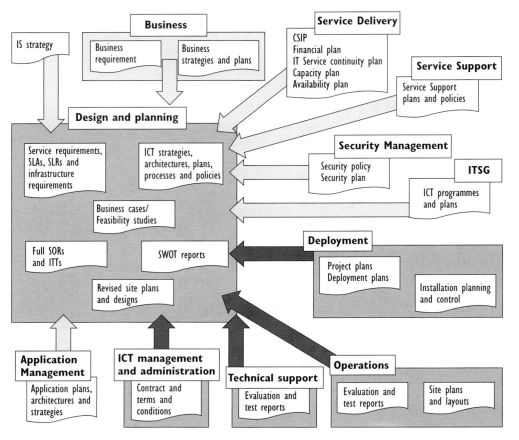

Figure B.2 – ITIL deliverables and interfaces

Making metrics work (BIP 0032)

Managing end-to-end service (BIP 0033)

Finance for service managers (BIP 0034)

Enabling change (BIP 0035)

Keeping the service going (BIP 0036)

Capacity management (BIP 0037)

Integrated service management (BIP 0038)

The differences between BS 15000 and ISO/IEC 20000 (BIP 0039)

This series provides practical guidance and advice on introducing IT Service Management best practice in accordance with ISO/IEC 20000.

Even though security issues are covered in ISO/IEC 20000-1, 6.6, the 'Achieving ISO/IEC 20000' series does not cover security issues. Information on security can be found in the BSI publications in the BIP 0070 series.

BSI security publications

BIP 0070, *Information security compilation on CD-ROM*

BIP 0071, *Information security management systems (ISMS) certification – Guidelines on requirements and preparation for certification based on ISO/IEC 27001:2005 (BS 7799-2:2005)*

BIP 0072, *Are you ready for a BS ISO/IEC 27001 information security management systems (ISMS) audit?*

BIP 0073, *Guide to the implementation and auditing of information security management systems (ISMS) controls*

BIP 0074, *Measuring the effectiveness of your ISMS implementations based on ISO/IEC 27001*

These publications provide the specification of requirements against which a service provider can be assessed and certified with regard to the quality of their IT management processes and system standards, advice on how to achieve the requirements, and additional information on all aspects of the requirements.

An ISO/IEC 20000 certification scheme based on an early BS 15000 certification scheme was introduced in 2006. The scheme was designed by the *it*SMF and is operated under their control. A number of auditing organisations are accredited within the scheme to assess and certify organisations against the standard.

A complementary book on Software Asset Management (SAM) has also been added to ITIL. This concentrates on the specific demands of managing software assets within an organisation and the related issues associated with the use of those software assets. The book definition states that 'SAM is all of the infrastructure and processes necessary for the effective management, control and protection of the software assets within an organisation, throughout all stages of their lifecycle'.

The overall objective of all SAM processes is good corporate governance, namely to manage, control and protect an organisation's software assets, including management of the risks arising from the use of those software assets.

The objective of the overall management processes is to establish and maintain the management infrastructure within which the other SAM processes are implemented. Each of the other process areas can then achieve their objectives as follows:

- **Core Asset Management processes:** to identify and maintain information about software assets throughout their lifecycle, and to manage physical assets related to software

- **Logistic processes:** to control all activities affecting the progress of software through its lifecycle
- **Verification and compliance processes:** to detect, escalate and manage all exceptions to SAM policies, processes, procedures and licence use rights
- **Relationship processes:** to manage all relationships within the business, and with partners and suppliers, to agreed contractual, legal and documented service terms and targets relating to the use of software.

B.5   ITIL update

OGC and its partners in ITIL are working together to improve the content of the publications and qualifications. The overwhelming driver for this refresh is to keep the guidance up to date such that ITIL continues to be 'fit for purpose' as the most widely accepted approach to IT Service Management in the world.

For more information, see www.itil.co.uk.

The new set of core books will follow a lifecycle model from design to retirement through five books. The titles are:

- Service Strategies
- Service Design
- Service Transition
- Service Operation
- Continual Service Improvement.

Appendix C COBIT

C.1 Purpose of COBIT

Over the past few decades, the use of IT in many organisations has grown dramatically and many business processes are dependent on IT for the delivery of service and control of information. Organisations must satisfy various legal requirements for their information, assets and client information while optimising the use of available IT resources. This requires the implementation of an IT governance framework to determine the level of governance and control required.

The Control Objectives for Information and related Technology (COBIT) 3rd Edition© was issued by the IT Governance Institute® (ITGI) in 2000. COBIT has delivered a generally accepted IT control framework enabling organisations to implement an IT governance control structure throughout the enterprise. Since its first issue in 1996, COBIT has been adopted in corporations and by governmental bodies throughout the world.

COBIT is 'business focused' ensuring that the delivery of IT services is aligned directly with business objectives and risks. This provides a clear definition of business imperatives by documenting the organisation's processes; routine issues are no longer hidden in the organisation, allowing IT to manage by exceptions. COBIT uses its heritage of management and audit experience to define many common processing exceptions and define these as part of the standard processes.

Recent corporate scandals have increased regulatory pressures on Boards of Directors to implement effective controls and report their status. This clearly affects IT controls, requiring organisations to improve IT performance, including the adoption of formal controls over their IT activities. IT managers, advisors and auditors have turned to COBIT as a basis for control. The COBIT framework meets the regulatory requirements of organisations by complying with various legal requirements including Sarbanes-Oxley (SOX). Consequently, COBIT is increasingly accepted as the standard response for assessing IT controls.

C.2 Description

Business orientation is the main theme of COBIT. It is designed to be employed not only by users and auditors, but also, and more importantly, as comprehensive guidance for management and business process owners. Increasingly, business practice involves the full empowerment of business process owners so they have total responsibility for all aspects of the business process. In particular, this includes providing adequate controls.

The CobiT framework provides a tool for the business process owner that facilitates the discharge of this responsibility. The framework starts from a simple and pragmatic premise:

> **In order to provide the information that the organisation requires to achieve its objectives, IT resources need to be managed by a set of naturally grouped processes.**

The framework continues with a set of 34 high-level control objectives, one for each of the IT processes, grouped into four domains:

- **Plan and Organise** – this domain covers strategy and tactics, and concerns the identification of the way IT can best contribute to the achievement of the business objectives. In addition, the realisation of the strategic vision needs to be planned, communicated and managed for different perspectives. Finally, a proper organisation as well as technological infrastructure must be put in place.

- **Acquire and Implement** – to realise the IT strategy, IT solutions need to be identified, developed or acquired, as well as implemented and integrated into the business process. In addition, changes in and maintenance of existing systems are covered by this domain to make sure that the lifecycle is continued for these systems.

- **Deliver and Support** – this domain is concerned with the actual delivery of required services, which range from traditional operations over security and continuity aspects, to training. In order to deliver services, the necessary support processes must be set up. This domain includes the actual processing of data by application systems, often classified under application controls.

- **Monitor and Evaluate** – all IT processes need to be regularly assessed over time for their quality and compliance with control requirements. This domain thus addresses management's oversight of the organisation's control process and independent assurance provided by internal and external audit or obtained from alternative sources.

In addition to the framework and control objectives, CobiT 3.0 consists of these components:

- **Executive Summary** – this provides a thorough awareness and understanding of CobiT's key concepts and principles and includes a synopsis of the framework, identifying CobiT's four domains and 34 IT processes.

- **Audit Guidelines** – corresponding to each of the 34 high-level control objectives is an audit guideline to enable the review of IT processes against CobiT's 318 recommended detailed control objectives to provide management assurance and/or advice for improvement.

- **Management Guidelines** – these guidelines further enhance and enable management to deal more effectively with the needs and requirements of IT governance. The guidelines are action-oriented and generic and provide management direction for getting the organisation's information and related processes under control, for monitoring achievement of organisational goals, for monitoring performance within each IT process and for benchmarking organisational achievement.

CobiT's management guidelines consist of maturity models, critical success factors (CSFs), key goal indicators (KGIs) and key performance indicators (KPIs). This structure delivers a significantly improved framework responding to management's need for control and measurability of IT by providing management with tools to assess and measure their organisation's IT environment against CobiT's 34 IT processes.

- **Implementation Toolset** – the toolset provides lessons learned from those organisations that have quickly and successfully applied CobiT in their work environments. It has two particularly useful tools – Management Awareness Diagnostic and IT Control Diagnostic – to assist in analysing an organisation's IT control environment.

For the purposes of CobiT, the following definitions are used:

- **Control** is defined as the policies, procedures, practices and organisational structures designed to provide reasonable assurance that business objectives will be achieved and that undesired events will be prevented or detected and corrected.

- **IT Control Objective** is a statement of the desired result or purpose to be achieved by implementing control procedures in a particular IT activity.

To satisfy business objectives, information needs to conform to certain criteria, which CobiT refers to as business requirements for information. In establishing the list of requirements, CobiT combines the principles embedded in existing and known reference models:

- **Quality requirements** – quality, cost, delivery
- **Fiduciary requirements** – effectiveness and efficiency of operations, reliability of information, compliance with laws and regulations
- **Security requirements** – confidentiality, integrity, availability.

Starting the analysis from the broader quality, fiduciary and security requirements, seven distinct, certainly overlapping, categories were extracted. CobiT's working definitions are as follows:

- **Effectiveness** deals with information being relevant and pertinent to the business process as well as being delivered in a timely, correct, consistent and usable manner.

- **Efficiency** concerns the provision of information through the optimal (most productive and economical) use of resources.

- **Confidentiality** concerns the protection of sensitive information from unauthorised disclosure.

- **Integrity** relates to the accuracy and completeness of information as well as to its validity in accordance with business values and expectations.

- **Availability** relates to information being available when required by the business process now and in the future. It also concerns the safeguarding of necessary resources and associated capabilities.

- **Compliance** deals with complying with those laws, regulations and contractual arrangements to which the business process is subject, i.e. externally imposed business criteria.

- **Reliability of information** relates to the provision of appropriate information for management to operate the entity and for management to exercise financial and compliance reporting responsibilities.

The IT resources identified in CobiT can be explained/defined as follows:

- **Data** are objects in their widest sense (i.e. external and internal), structured and unstructured, graphics, sound, etc.

- **Application systems** are understood to be the sum of manual and programmed procedures.

- **Technology** covers hardware, operating systems, database management systems, networking, multimedia, etc.

- **Facilities** are all the resources to house and support information systems.

- **People** include staff skills, awareness and productivity to plan, organise, acquire, deliver, support, monitor and evaluate information systems and services.

C.3 How to implement CobiT

The Implementation Toolkit (described above) is the starting point for implementing CobiT.

In recent years, the CobiT library has expanded to include several supporting and specific-focus publications, such as:

- *Control Practices* – these expand the capabilities of CobiT by providing the practitioner with an additional level of detail. The CobiT IT processes, business requirements and detailed control objectives define *the tasks that need to be executed* to implement an effective control structure. The control practices provide the more detailed *how* and *why* needed by management, service providers, end-users and control professionals to implement highly specific controls based on an analysis of operational and IT risks.

- CoBIT *Online*® – this is the online version of CoBIT designed to allow for immediate access to the CoBIT content. For each of the 34 IT processes, the user can read the framework wording, then select any one of the navigation buttons to read the detailed control objective, audit guideline, key goal indicators, key performance indicators, critical success factors and maturity model associated with it. Users can apply filters to create their own customised version of CoBIT. Benchmarking and a community section allow for comparison and sharing of experience.

- CoBIT *Quickstart*™ – this version of CoBIT is a baseline for small to medium enterprises (SMEs) and other entities where IT is not mission-critical or essential for survival. It can also serve as a starting point for other organisations in their move towards an appropriate level of control and governance of IT. This publication was developed in response to comments that CoBIT, in its complete form, can be rather overwhelming. CoBIT Quickstart constitutes a practical subset of the entire CoBIT volume. Only those control objectives that are considered the most critical are included, so that implementation of CoBIT's fundamental principles can take place easily, effectively and relatively quickly.

- CoBIT *Security Baseline* – this version extracts the security-related control objectives and offers a basic understanding of information security, a control baseline for security and 'survival kits' consisting of essential awareness messages for differing audiences.

CoBIT provides good practices for the management of IT processes in a logical structure, meeting the multiple needs of enterprise management by balancing business risks, technical issues, control needs and performance measurement requirements. Emphasis is placed on the increasingly important role of IT governance and the emerging application of Balanced Scorecards to organisations' IT activities. Much of CoBIT is available as a complimentary download from the IT Governance Institute website, www.itgi.org.

CoBIT 4.0 simplifies the presentation of the CoBIT framework and resources by combining the executive summary, the framework, control objectives and resources from the management guidelines into a single reference. The structure of this resource is explained in Chapter 3, IT governance. The changes introduced in CoBIT 4.0 improve the links with ITIL Service Management processes and introduce new guidelines for aligning IT processes with business objectives and responsibilities. CoBIT 4.0 is seen as an addition to the CoBIT resources, not a replacement for CoBIT 3.0. This is important because many organisations have already established successful risk/control solutions based on CoBIT 3.0.

C.4   CobiT and ITIL

The best practices emerging are using CobiT as a governance framework with ITIL. By taking the critical success factors, key performance indicators and maturity models from the CobiT control objectives and matching this to the ITIL processes an excellent implementation of best practice can be achieved.

To support the alignment of CobiT and ITIL the starting point is the alignment of the CobiT control objectives to the ITIL processes. More details of a joint project to provide initial guidance are available at www.itil.co.uk/includes/ITIL-COBiT.pdf.

Appendix D ISO/IEC 20000

D.1 Introduction

ISO/IEC 20000 is the first international standard for Service Management. It specifies best practices for management responsibilities and Service Management within an overall Plan-Do-Check-Act (PDCA) cycle. Service providers can use the standard to give them an understanding of best practice Service Management. The standard is also an objective benchmark of management processes. Service providers should be able to reduce risks to their customer's business activities and deliver better services more cost-effectively by achieving ISO/IEC 20000.

D.2 The origins of the standard

ISO/IEC 20000 was based on BS 15000, the first formal national standard for Service Management. It was developed by BDD/3, Service management, a British Standards Institution (BSI) committee.

The BSI's work on the standard started in 1989, with publication of a basic code of practice in 1995. This gave advice on four Service Management processes. In 1998, a second edition of the code of practice was published. This gave advice on 13 Service Management processes.

At this stage priority was given to the development of a standard that was suitable for certification audits. A code of practice is unsuitable for certification audits as a code of practice gives advice. Audits are based on a specification that lists compulsory requirements. As a result, a two-part standard was produced. One part was Edition 1 of a new specification, worded to be suitable for audits. The other part was the original code of practice enhanced and updated to provide advice on achieving the requirements in the specification. At this stage, the name 'BS 15000' was allocated.

D.3 The BS 15000 series

Plans also took into account what else was required to convert a national standard into an international standard. This included the production of supporting publications to give a full BS 15000 series.

Two other publications were produced as supporting material for the standard. One publication was a self-assessment workbook for use in internal quality checks on process quality. The other publication was *A Managers' Guide to Service Management* as an introduction to ITIL and to BS 15000. These both used a less formal style and language than is allowed in standards.

As later editions of BS 15000 were produced and now ISO/IEC 20000, this material has been updated to reflect the changes.

D.4   The Early Adopters scheme

Proposing a national standard as the basis for an international equivalent is more likely to be acceptable if the standard has been tried, tested and improved on the basis of practical experience. The BS 15000 series, including BS 15000, was used for an Early Adopters' scheme in 2001. In this scheme a representative sample of organisations tested the publications in the BS 15000 series. Advice from Early Adopters was used to improve the standard and led to Edition 2 of Part 1 being produced in 2002, and of Part 2 in 2003.

D.5   Conversion to become a management system standard

The key difference between Editions 1 and 2 of the standard was the inclusion of management responsibilities, including the Plan-Do-Check-Act cycle. This aligned BS 15000 with other management system standards, such as the ISO 9000 'family', although the ISO 9000 family and BS 15000 standards were separate. The two sets of standards remain separate, even though ISO/IEC 20000 is now also an international standard and what was ISO 9000-3 has become ISO/IEC 90003.

D.6   BS 15000 certification

The second edition of BS 15000 was considered sufficiently mature to be the basis of certification audits. In June 2003 the *it*SMF launched a scheme that assessed the quality of Accredited Certification Bodies (informally referred to as a 'professional audit company'). If these organisations meet the *it*SMF's quality criteria they may become an *it*SMF Registered Certification Body (RCB). An RCB may use the *it*SMF certification scheme logo on certificates awarded following a successful audit.

By early 2004 several organisations had achieved BS 15000 certification audits and many more were planned, with much greater interest outside the UK than had been expected by this stage.

Training schemes for auditors, consultants and practitioners had also been established, providing a base of skills for the take-up of an international version of BS 15000.

D.7 Fast-tracking to ISO/IEC 20000

BS 15000 was an established as a national standard that was being used internationally. This encouraged the BSI to submit both parts of BS 15000 to become an international standard, via a fast-track process.

The fast-track process took less than 14 months, starting in November 2004. The process included discussion and voting by national standard bodies. The vote announced in May 2004 was in favour of acceptance. A few months were required to resolve comments and agreed changes, final editing and reformatting. ISO/IEC 20000 was published on 15 December 2005.

The UK implementation, BS ISO/IEC 20000, was also published and BS 15000 withdrawn on the same date. The UK implementation includes a national foreword and a national annex, but otherwise the documents are identical to their ISO/IEC equivalents. The BSI has included references to ITIL in the national annex that are not otherwise allowed in an ISO/IEC standard, which only allows references to ISO and ISO/IEC standards.

D.8 The differences

There are 450 differences between BS 15000 and ISO/IEC 20000, but over 400 of the differences are minor changes to the structure, format or small wording changes to clarify the meaning, particularly for readers who do not have English as a first language. There were fewer than 20 changes to requirements.

D.9 What the standard provides

The standard is viewed across the industry as a crucial step in turning best practice potential into reality. Compliance requirements for management systems, service planning, process relationships, Service Delivery, resolution, relationships, control and release processes are set out.

The standard is playing an increasingly important role in governance and the meeting of legal and regulatory requirements. It is also increasingly being required of commercial service suppliers as part of the tendering process and in contracts.

Another key factor is the alignment with other management system standards such as the ISO 9000 family and ISO/IEC 27001. The interaction between the management system responsibilities and Service Management processes is one of the bigger benefits of the standard.

Achieving ISO/IEC 20000 drives out additional benefits often not obtained if a service management process is implemented in isolation of others. This is because the standard requires:

- genuine management commitment to best practices
- that interfaces between processes and organisations are understood and managed
- that processes are integrated.

Achieving ISO/IEC 20000 also means that variants in processes that are unjustified are eliminated. This reduces risks and improves efficiency.

One of the main drivers during the drafting of BS 15000 and ISO/IEC 20000 was that achieving the requirements should improve efficiency and effectiveness. Meeting requirements by adding a bureaucratic and unnecessary overhead means the service provider has failed to understand ISO/IEC 20000. Understanding that ISO/IEC 20000 is about 'doing not documenting' simplifies the improvements, reducing the cost of achieving the requirements and making it easier to improve in the future.

D.10   ISO/IEC 20000 certification

Conformance with ISO/IEC 20000 is based on conformance with BS 15000, following updating of audit guidelines and auditor training, to allow for the differences in requirements between BS 15000 and ISO/IEC 20000.

It is increasingly recognised that at a minimum, before an external certification audit, a service provider will have been engaged in:

- establishing management commitment, accountability and roles
- agreeing the scope of Service Management
- drafting a scope statement for an audit
- assessment of current practice
- comparison of practices with ISO/IEC 20000 requirements
- documentation of gaps and overlaps
- planning improvements such as new processes
- implementation of changes to achieve compliance
- plans for maintaining compliance through continual improvement.

Regulations that apply to the audit industry do not allow the same organisation to give advice on ISO/IEC 20000 to a service provider and then to audit them against ISO/IEC 20000, as is the case for all other standards.

As with any certification audit, an organisation that is interested in achieving

ISO/IEC 20000, or who wishes to rely on a supplier's ISO/IEC 20000 certificate should carefully check the credentials of the prospective supplier. Will the prospective auditor use staff trained in Service Management or will they allocate staff who have only had experience with other management system standards or with specialist technical standards? Will they check the reality of practices or restrict their audit to an examination of documents and records? Will the potential auditor recognise and respect the compulsory nature of the Part 1 requirements, or will they allow a scope statement for the audit that is 'pick and mix' with compulsory requirements treated as if they were optional? Are they claiming to be an accredited certification body when they are not? In the latter case the organisation may be perfectly competent to do a pre-audit review or readiness review, but the certification will not have the same credibility.

Not all service providers pass an audit without any deficiencies being found and a good audit company will be able to provide constructive comments on how to resolve each recorded deficiency. A good audit company will also check that there is real management commitment to best practices, that there is a logical relationship between policy, process and procedure and that processes are understood and integrated. This drives many of the real benefits of achieving ISO/IEC 20000.

Conversely, a bad audit company, for example one that checks only documents, will drive the service provider being audited towards a 'documenting not doing' approach, with a bureaucratic overhead adding costs and not value. In these circumstances excessive numbers of long documents are a contrary indicator, not a sign of best practices.

D.11 Tools and products

As ISO/IEC 20000 is a standard for processes so use of Service Management tools is not included in requirements. In practice, a service provider will be very limited in what can be achieved without some tools. Tools should be suitable for the service provider's circumstances. Typically a small service provider needs simpler tools than a large service provider, particularly where a service provider (or the customer's organisation) is split across many locations.

Product providers centre their process improvement products initially in the assessment, comparison, documenting and planning of continual improvement, and later in the implementation and maintenance phases of the programme. The majority will use ITIL to assist them in this.

D.12 ITIL and ISO/IEC 20000 alignment

In 1996 the policy was adopted of aligning BS 15000 and ITIL, under an agreement with the owners of ITIL copyright and with the support of *it*SMF-UK.

This policy of alignment between the two has continued through each new edition and is included in the current work referred to as 'ITIL Refresh', which is updating and improving ITIL Edition 2.

It is also worth noting that although it is much easier to achieve ISO/IEC 20000 if ITIL advice has been intelligently adopted and adapted, there is no reference to ITIL in the requirement or recommendations. This apparent anomaly is a result of the difference between a standard, which specifies compulsory requirements, and the advice in ITIL, which is optional and includes alternative approaches. A standard specifies what must be achieved and ITIL gives greater emphasis on how it is to be achieved. The rules of how standards are written also prevent inclusion of a requirement to 'adopt ITIL'.

Although only a tiny proportion of service providers have considered aiming for ISO/IEC 20000 without adopting and adapting ITIL, some have used terms that do not match exactly those in ITIL. This is acceptable for an ISO/IEC 20000 audit.

D.13 The future of ISO/IEC 20000

The standard is now managed by an international committee, ISO/IEC JTC-1/SC 7, which established Work Group 25 to be responsible for ISO/IEC 20000.

ISO/IEC JTC-1 is a joint committee formed by ISO (International Organization for Standardization) and IEC (International Electrotechnical Commission). It includes in its scope all IT-related standards, such as ISO/IEC 27001, ISO/IEC 17799 and ISO/IEC 90003. (Development of generic quality standards such as ISO 9000 is managed by a separate international committee under different rules.)

The group responsible for ISO/IEC 20000 is composed of representatives of approximately 45 national standards bodies. The rules governing ISO/IEC JTC-1 committees also allow international organisations to become involved in discussions. *it*SMF International had been accepted by JTC-1 at the time this book was published.

Also at the time of publication of this book enhancements to ISO/IEC 20000 were being discussed, following the normal standards development route and not the fast-track process used to convert BS 15000 to an international standard. Commitments to the following improvements were made during fast-tracking:

- advice on scoping and applicability (Part 3)
- better alignment between the details of Part 2 compared to Part 1
- harmonisation with other international standards and vocabulary while recognising the benefits of the alignment between ITIL and the standard.

Appendix E QUALITY MANAGEMENT

E.1 Purpose

The management of quality is a key issue for all organisations. Quality management for IT services is a logical way of ensuring that all the activities necessary to design, develop and implement IT services which satisfy the requirements of the organisation and of users, take place as planned and that the activities are carried out cost-effectively.

There are so many experts or 'gurus' on the subject of quality management that it can all seem very mystifying. In reality, it is the use of common sense rather than a complex intellectual subject.

A Quality Management System (QMS) specifies the way that an organisation plans to manage its operations so that it delivers quality services. The QMS defines the organisational structure, responsibilities, policies, procedures, processes, standards and resources required to deliver quality IT services. However, a QMS will only function as intended if the top management and staff are committed to achieving its objectives.

This appendix gives brief details on a number of different quality approaches and also identifies industry recognition opportunities for quality management – more detail on these and other approaches can be found on the Internet at www.dti.gov.uk/quality.

E.2 Description

E.2.1 Quality improvement: the Deming Cycle

W. Edwards Deming is best known for his management philosophy for establishing quality, productivity and competitive position. As part of this philosophy, he formulated 14 points of attention for managers. Some of these points are more appropriate to Service Management than others.

For quality improvement, Deming proposed the Deming Cycle or Circle. The four key stages are 'Plan, Do, Check and Act' after which a phase of consolidation prevents the 'Circle' from 'rolling down the hill' as illustrated in Figure E.1.

The cycle is underpinned by a process-led approach to management where defined processes are in place, the activities measured for compliance to expected values and outputs audited to validate and improve the process.

More information on Deming and his theories can be found at www.deming.org.

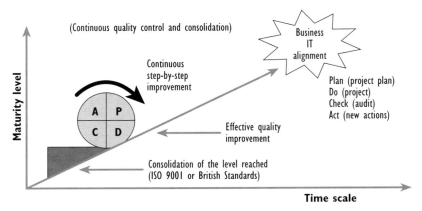

Figure E.1 – The Deming Cycle

E.2.2   Formal quality initiatives

Quality Standards: International Organization for Standardization (ISO) 9001:2000 Quality Management System – Requirements

ISO 9001:2000 is a set of generic quality-based guidelines that apply to all types of organisations and is accepted worldwide. It does not matter what size they are or what they do. It can help product-, process- and service-based organisations achieve standards of quality that are recognised and respected throughout the world.

The year 2000 version of the standard is used as a basis for good business management in a wider sense, and recognises that efficient processes, developing people, and continual improvement leading to customer satisfaction help meet key business objectives.

It follows the basic principles of 'Say what you do, do what you say' and looks to improve business processes and achieve higher levels of customer satisfaction. A third-party assessment body can be contracted to certify an organisation's Quality Management System to ISO 9001:2000 to assure the customer that the company operates an effective business management system.

The standard uses eight business principles that reflect current business management to allow an improved response to customers' needs and expectations. The eight principles are:

■ customer-focused organisation

■ leadership

■ involvement of people

■ process approach

■ systematic approach to management

■ continual improvement

- factual approach to decision-making
- promotion of supplier partnerships.

The senior management of an organisation 'owns' the Quality Management System. These people are responsible for developing quality objectives (or key performance indicators) and the process responsibilities.

IT Service Management (the ISO/IEC 20000 series)

This series of standards is described in Appendix D.

Total Quality Systems: The EFQM Excellence Model

The presidents of 14 major European companies, with the endorsement of the European Commission, founded the European Foundation for Quality Management (EFQM) in 1988. The present membership is in excess of 600 well-respected organisations, ranging from major multinationals and important national companies to research institutes in prominent European universities.

The Excellence Model's key benefits are that it:

- promotes a focused leadership
- increases the involvement of people
- creates an action plan framework to improve processes
- provides strong links to the business planning process
- gives a quantified measure of moving forward.

Whereas ISO 9001:2000 focuses on 'good process management', the model provides a direction for those wishing to achieve business 'excellence' through a programme of continual improvement. It consists of nine criteria and 32 sub-criteria and follows the 'Plan-Do-Check-Act' cycle and the need to direct everything that is processed, monitored and measured to the goals of the business.

This model does not tell organisations what they need to do. However, it does provide guidelines to promote the thinking behind 'being the best'. The first five criteria are defined as 'enablers', with the second set defined as 'results'. Best practice in ITIL process implementations shows that placing proper emphasis on these topics increases the chances for success. The nine criteria it considers are:

- leadership
- people
- policy and strategy
- partnerships and resources
- processes
- people results

- customer results
- society results
- key performance indicators.

One of the advantages of this model is that it can be used without using a third-party assessor. Most organisations know their processes, subsequent strengths and areas for improvement. The model provides a useful self-assessment questionnaire as part of its toolkit. When a self-assessment is undertaken, an organisation reviews both what it does and what it achieves using a combination of people's perceptions and information from monitoring and measuring exercises used in its daily activities.

There are seven basic steps to using the Excellence Model. The organisation can decide the best approach and management techniques based upon the 'common approach' in the organisation:

- **Step 1:** Gain and develop commitment of the top management in the application and use of self-assessment
- **Step 2:** Select and plan the self-assessment approach
- **Step 3:** Select and train the right people to perform the self-assessment
- **Step 4:** Determine the right way to communicate the self-assessment plans to a wide and differing audience
- **Step 5:** Perform the self-assessment
- **Step 6:** Review, prioritise, own and set SMART targets for the identified improvement opportunities
- **Step 7:** Identify resources and initiate improvement teams to monitor and measure implementation actions.

Self-assessment can score up to 1000 points although this is extremely unlikely to ever be achieved. A score of around 300 points is a reasonable performance and it is estimated that less than 5% of UK-based organisations score over 500 points. 'Excellence' organisations may score between 700 and 800 points and still be able to identify improvement areas.

Six Sigma

Quality management and business excellence models are common approaches to continuous improvement. These concepts will assist an organisation in reaching its objectives and exceeding them. However, Six Sigma, whilst closely linked with improvement concepts, is a quality tool and differs in that the focus is very much more on the end result through its concentrated use.

Six Sigma is a data-driven approach to analysing the root causes of problems and solving them. This method concentrates on the process capability for customer-specified products and services and how to supply them quicker and in a more cost-effective manner.

How does it do this? By analysing the 'value-added' parts of the process and reducing costs that do not add value to the customer. This is not just about cost cutting. Six Sigma ensures reduced costs while maintaining or improving value to the customer.

In statistical terms, actual Six Sigma performance equates to 3.4 defects per million process or service opportunities. Achieving this variability reduction for the majority of processes is a challenging task. The methodology follows through a define-measure-analyse-improve-control process, which is based on the Deming Cycle.

- Define the scope and goals of the improvement project in terms of customer requirements and the process that delivers these requirements.

- Measure the current process performance, process inputs and outputs – and calculate the process capability.

- Identify and analyse the gap between the current and required performance, identifying and prioritising causes and effects of problems. It is at this stage where benchmarking of the results against recognised standards of performance can be used.

- Generate the improvement solutions and fixing problems to prevent them from reoccurring so that the required financial and other performance goals are met.

- Control implementation of the improved process in a way that maintains the improvements. Any new or revised procedures will be documented in the Quality Management System with performance targets monitored and measured regularly. After a 'running-in' period, the process capability can be calculated once again to establish whether the performance gains are being sustained. If not, the cycle process will need to be repeated.

Six Sigma is not a 'one-off' process. It needs to be supported in a culture that invests in process improvement. Trained specialists (with grades up to 'black belts') should provide the necessary knowledge and technical capability to identify opportunities and lead the attack on delivering breakthroughs in performance that affect the 'bottom line'.

Six Sigma is the driver for achieving business excellence. Its roots can be found with Total Quality Management (TQM), which looks at long-term quality benefits as the programme begins to change hearts and minds. Six Sigma is about delivering benefits now through an intense controlled effort. Service Management support tools, including tracking of incidents, etc., would allow this approach to be used for process improvement.

E.2.3 Quality awards

The European Quality Award

To demonstrate a successful application of the EFQM model using the nine stated criteria, some organisations aim for the European Quality Award. This is a rigorous and demanding contest, designed for organisations, or organisational units, seen as national and European role models with a five-year history of continuous improvement. More details on the award can be viewed at www.efqm.org.

The Malcolm Baldrige Quality Award

The US equivalent to the European award is the Malcolm Baldrige Quality Award for Quality Management. The Malcolm Baldrige National Quality Improvement Act of 1987 established an annual US National Quality Award. The purpose of the award was (and still is) to promote awareness of quality excellence, to recognise quality achievements of US companies, and to publicise successful quality strategies.

The US Commerce Department's National Institute of Standards and Technology (NIST) manages the Baldrige National Quality Program in close cooperation with the private sector.

The Baldrige performance excellence criteria are a framework that any organisation can use to improve overall performance. Seven categories make up the award criteria:

- leadership
- strategic planning
- customer and market focus
- information and analysis
- human resource focus
- process management
- business results.

The basic purposes of the award are to promote recognition of quality achievements and to raise awareness of the importance and techniques of quality improvement. In summary, the award:

- focuses more on results and service
- relies upon the involvement of many different professional and trade groups
- provides special credits for innovative approaches to quality
- includes a strong customer and human resource focus
- stresses the importance of sharing information
- focuses on process management.

More details are available at www.quality.nist.gov.

Appendix F RISK MANAGEMENT

F.1 Overview

As highlighted in the chapters throughout this book, risk management is an inherent ingredient in any well-managed organisation. The importance is reflected in current legislation and regulatory requirements (Basel II are regulatory guidelines – CAD 3 is legislation), which require risk management to be demonstrable in terms of methods and responsibility for managing risk.

This appendix provides a reference to key regulations, drivers and best practice with regard to risk management. While the details shown below are primarily focused on UK-listed companies and large financial organisations, practices based on reports such as Turnbull are being used voluntarily by public sector, smaller and non-PLC organisations, to improve and also demonstrate the quality of an organisation, to existing and new clients, and other stakeholders in the business.

Clearly, different regulations are in operation within countries throughout the world. However, Basel II and Sarbanes-Oxley (SOX) are becoming *de facto* standards. Many will be based on or have similar requirements to those identified here. Further information can be obtained from the websites detailed in the Bibliography (Chapter 10).

F.2 Code for listed companies in the UK

Turnbull Guidance – incorporated into the Listing Rule disclosure requirements of the London Stock Exchange. This means that non-compliance with the Turnbull Guidance would result in an embarrassing disclosure in the annual report, which could attract media attention, shareholder activists and institutional investors. The guidance relates to companies listed on the London Stock Exchange but is voluntarily adopted by a number of non-listed organisations as well. The guidance is about the adoption of a risk-based approach to establishing a system of internal control and reviewing its effectiveness.

The Combined Code on Corporate Governance 2003 – superseding the combined code issued by the Hampel Committee in 1998, requires listed companies to make a disclosure statement in two parts, the first stating how it applies the principles in the code, the second to either confirm that it complies or where it does not comply. This revision is based on the recommendations set out in the Higgs Report and the Smith Report on audit committees published in January 2003.

F.3   UK Financial Services Authority (FSA)

FSA – Integrated Prudential Sourcebook (PRU) – SYSC 3A (high-level Sourcebook 'Senior Management Arrangements, Systems and Controls') 6.2 and 6.3 relates to Expected Changes and states that 'before, during and after a significant change to its organisation, infrastructure or business operating environment, a firm should assess and monitor how this change will affect its risk profile and should establish and maintain appropriate systems and controls for the management of the risks involved in expected changes'.

F.4   Code for listed companies in the US

Sarbanes-Oxley (SOX) – passed by law in the US in 2002 for adoption by the end of 2004 and, as with the Combined Code in the UK, relates to listed companies. SOX was developed in response to a number of major corporate and accounting scandals involving prominent companies in the United States. These scandals resulted in a loss of public trust in accounting and reporting practices. SOX compliance requires the defining of a risk management process that can be used to identify risks early, and to plan mitigation strategies. In addition, project management areas are also identified, including implementing a standard project management process to establish control processes and activities associated with scope, cost and schedule, and to establish a project category or classification scheme that includes all projects associated or impacted with Sarbanes-Oxley compliance. It is expected that SOX will, over time, have a wider reach and impact internationally, rather than simply being confined to companies having a US listing.

F.5   Regulation for the banking sector worldwide

Basel II – The Basel II Capital Accord – the Accord was developed by the banking regulators from the G-10 countries (the G-10 is actually 11 countries: Belgium, Canada, France, Germany, Italy, Japan, the Netherlands, Sweden, Switzerland, the United Kingdom and the United States) and Luxembourg, which formed a standing committee under the auspices of the Bank for International Settlements (BIS). Called the Basel Committee on Banking Supervision, the committee comprises representatives from central banks and regulatory authorities.

The Basel Committee does not have legislative authority, but participant countries are implicitly bound to implement its recommendations. Usually, the committee has allowed for some flexibility in how local authorities implement recommendations, so national laws vary.

In 1988, the Basel Committee proposed a set of minimal capital requirements for banks. These became law in G-10 countries in 1992, with Japanese banks permitted an extended transition period. The requirements have come to be known as the 1988 Basel Accord.

In January 1999, the Basel Committee proposed a new capital accord, which has come to be known as Basel II. There followed an extensive consultative period, with the committee releasing additional proposals for consultation in January 2001 and April 2003. The finalised Basel II Accord was released in June 2004.

The Basel II Accord requires all internationally active banks, at every tier within the banking group, to adopt similar or consistent risk management practices for tracking and publicly reporting exposure to operational, credit and market risks. Included in the Basel Accord is a requirement regarding having sufficient capital in the balance sheet to support the level of business being conducted, taking into account the level of risk related to the various business activities. It is along the same principles as Basel I but with the added concept of recognising that different types and levels of risk may require different levels of capital, i.e. if you have £1 (say) on the balance sheet you can only do £100 (say) of trade, known as capital adequacy, to cover the negative manifestation of risk to a financial institution. From a regulatory perspective, this is also to protect against systemic risk, whereby the effect of a major financial institution not being able to meet its obligations could cause a domino effect impacting the finance sector as a whole. The new Accord is due to take effect from 2006, and many financial organisations have been developing processes and capturing data for some time in preparation for the compliance.

F.6   Approach to risk – best practice

There are a number of approaches and guides relating to risk management. Not all have been listed here, but further details can be found at the website addresses referenced.

The Office of Government Commerce (OGC) Management of Risk: Guidance aims to provide assistance to organisations wanting to put in place effective frameworks for management of risk. The guidance provides a series of approaches with checklists and pointers to more detailed sources of information. The approach described in the guide complements OGC's guidance on programme (MSP) and project (PRINCE2) management, and is continually updated to reflect best practice. The approach, branded by OGC as M_o_R, is supported by training and qualifications available from Accredited Training Organisations (see Chapter 10, Bibliography).

M_o_R details the following critical success factors for management of risk to be effective:

- senior management to support, own and lead on risk management
- risk management policies and the benefits of effective management clearly communicated to all staff

- the existence and adoption of a framework for management of risk (as shown above), that is transparent and repeatable
- the existence of an organisational culture which is supported through risk taking and innovation
- management of risk fully embedded in management processes and consistently applied
- risk associated with working with other organisations explicitly assessed and managed
- risk actively monitored and regularly reviewed on a constructive no-blame basis.

A series of checklists provided in the M_o_R Guide can be used, from different perspectives, to assess how well your organisation is managing risk.

F.7 In summary

There are many reasons for applying effective risk management within business, including the requirements from regulation and compliance. However, there are positive drivers for adopting risk management, including demonstrating the quality and investment potential of an organisation and as stated by a senior member of the public sector *'the benefits to any business of a sound risk management approach identified that, ironically, more risks can be taken when given the comfort of well-controlled framework, thus achieving greater reward for the business and its shareholders'*.

INDEX

NB: Page numbers in **bold** refer to figures.

Best Practice:
the OGC approach with ITIL® and PRINCE®

OGC Best Practice is an approach to management challenges as well as the application of techniques and actions.

Practical, flexible and adaptable, management guidance from OGC translates the very best of the world's practices into guidance of an internationally recognised standard. Both PRINCE2 and ITIL publications can help every organisation to:

* Run projects more efficiently
* Reduce project risk
* Purchase IT more cost effectively
* Improve organisational Service Delivery.

What is ITIL and why use it?

ITIL's starting point is that organisations do not simply use IT; they depend on it. Managing IT as effectively as possible must therefore be a high priority.

ITIL consists of a unique library of guidance on providing quality IT services. It focuses tightly on the customer, cost effectiveness and building a culture that puts the emphasis on IT performance.

Used by hundreds of the world's most successful organisations, its core titles are available in print, Online Subscription and CD-ROM formats. They are:

* Service Support
* Service Delivery
* Planning to Implement Service Management
* Application Management
* ICT Infrastructure Management
* Security Management
* The Business Perspective Volume 1 and 2
* Software Asset Management

What is PRINCE2 and why use it?

Since its introduction in 1989, PRINCE has been widely adopted by both the public and private sectors and is now recognised as a de facto standard for project management – and for the management of change.

PRINCE2, the most evolved version, is driven by its experts and users to offer control, transparency, focus and ultimate success for any project you need to implement.

Publications are available in various formats: print, Online Subscription and CD-ROM. Its main titles are:

* Managing Successful Projects with PRINCE2
* People Issues and PRINCE2
* PRINCE2 Pocket Book
* Tailoring PRINCE2
* Business Benefits through Project Management

Other related titles:
* Passing the PRINCE2 Examinations
* Managing Successful Programmes
* Management of Risk – Guidance for Practitioners
* Buying Software – A best practice approach

Ordering

The full range of ITIL and PRINCE2 publications can be purchased direct via **www.get-best-practice.co.uk** or through calling TSO Customer Services on **0870 600 5522**. If you are outside of the UK please contact your local agent, for details email **sales@tso.co.uk** For information on Network Licenses for CD-ROM and Online Subscription please email **network.sales@tso.co.uk**

You are also able to subscribe to content online through this website or by calling TSO Customer Services on **0870 600 5522**. For more information on how to subscribe online please refer to our help pages on the website.

Other Information Sources and Services

The IT Service Management Forum (itSMF)

The IT Service Management Forum Ltd (itSMF) is the only internationally recognised and independent body dedicated to IT Service Management. It is a not-for-profit organisation, wholly owned, and principally operated, by its membership.

The itSMF is a major influence on, and contributor to, Industry Best Practice and Standards worldwide, working in partnership with OGC (the owners of ITIL), the British Standards Institution (BSI), the Information Systems Examination Board (ISEB) and the Examination Institute of the Netherlands (EXIN).

Founded in the UK in 1991, there are now a number of chapters around the world with new ones seeking to join all the time. There are well in excess of 1000 organisations covering over 10,000 individuals represented in the membership. Organisations range from large multi-nationals such as AXA, GuinnessUDV, HP, Microsoft and Procter & Gamble in all market sectors, through central & local bodies, to independent consultants.

How to contact us:

The IT Service Management Forum Ltd
Webbs Court
8 Holmes Road
Earley
Reading RG6 7BH
Tel: +44 (0) 118 926 0888
Fax: +44 (0) 118 926 3073
Email: service@itsmf.com
or visit our web-site at:
www.itsmf.com

ITIL training and professional qualifications

There are currently two examining bodies offering equivalent qualifications: ISEB (The Information Systems Examining Board), part of the British Computer Society, and Stitching EXIN (The Netherlands Examinations Institute). Jointly with OGC and itSMF (the IT Service Management Forum), they work to ensure that a common standard is adopted for qualifications worldwide. The syllabus is based on the core elements of ITIL and complies with ISO9001 Quality Standard. Both ISEB and EXIN also accredit training organisations to deliver programmes leading to qualifications.

For further information:

visit ISEB's web-site at:
www.bcs.org.uk

and EXIN:
www.exin.nl

Dear customer ■ ■ ■ ■ ■ ■ ■ ■ ■ ■ ▦ ▦ ▦ ▦ ▦

We would like to hear from you with any comments or suggestions that you have on how we can improve our current products or develop new ones for the ITIL series. Please complete this questionnaire and we will enter you into our quarterly draw. The winner will receive a copy of Software Asset Management worth £35!

1 Personal Details

Name ....

Organisation ....

Job Title ....

Department ....

Address ....

....

Postcode ....

Telephone Number ....

Email ....

2 Nature of Organisation (tick one box only)

☐ Consultancy/Training
☐ Computing/IT/Software
☐ Industrial
☐ Central Government
☐ Local Government
☐ Academic/Further education
☐ Private Health
☐ Public Health (NHS)
☐ Finance
☐ Construction
☐ Telecommunications
☐ Utilities
☐ Other (Please specify)

....

3 How did you hear about ITIL?

☐ Work/Colleagues
☐ Internet/Web (please specify)

....

☐ Marketing Literature
☐ itSMF
☐ Other (please specify)

....

4 Where did you purchase this book?

☐ Web – www.tso.co.uk/bookshop
☐ Web – www.get-best-practice.co.uk
☐ Web – Other (please specify)

....

☐ Bookshop (please specify)

....

☐ Training Course
☐ Other (please specify)

....

5 How many people use ITIL in your company?

☐ 1-5
☐ 6-10
☐ 11-50
☐ 51-200
☐ 201+

6 How many people use your copy of this title?

☐ 0
☐ 1-5
☐ 6-10
☐ 11+

7 Overall, how do you rate this title?

☐ Excellent
☐ Very Good
☐ Good
☐ Fair
☐ Poor

8 What do you most like about the book? (tick all that apply)

☐ Ease of use
☐ Well structured
☐ Contents
☐ Index
☐ Hints and tips
☐ Other (Please specify)

....

9 Do you have any suggestions for improvement?

....

....

....

....

10 How do you use this book? (tick all that apply)

☐ Problem Solver
☐ Reference
☐ Tutorial
☐ Other (please specify)

....

[PTO]

11 Did you know there are 7 core titles in the **ITIL** series?

☐ No
☐ Yes

12 Do you have any other **ITIL** titles?

☐ No
☐ Yes (please specify)

....

13 Do you use the **ITIL** CDs?

☐ No
☐ Yes (please specify)

....

14 Are you aware that most of the **ITIL** series is now available as online content at **www.get-best-practice.co.uk?**

☐ Yes
☐ No

15 Do you currently subscribe to any online content found at **www.get-best-practice.co.uk?**

☐ No
☐ Yes (please specify)

....

16 Did you know that you can network your CDs and Online Subscription, to offer your project managers access to this material at their desktop?

Yes/No

☐ Please tick this box if you require further information.

17 Did you know that you are able to purchase a maintenance agreement for your CD-ROM that will allow you to receive immediately any revised versions, at no additional cost?

Yes/No

☐ Please tick this box if you require further information.

18 What business change guidance/methods does your company use?

☐ PRINCE2
☐ Managing Successful Programmes
☐ Management of Risk
☐ Successful Delivery Toolkit
☐ Business Systems Development (BSD)
☐ Other (please specify)

....

19 What is the job title of the person who makes the decision to implement **ITIL** and/or purchase IT?

....

....

20 Which three websites do you visit the most?

1 ....

2 ....

3 ....

21 Which 3 professional magazines do you read the most?

1 ....

2 ....

3 ....

22 Will you be attending any events or conferences this year related to IT, if so, which?

....

To enter your Questionnaire into our monthly draw please return this form to our Freepost Address:

Marketing – ITIL Questionnaire
TSO
Freepost ANG4748
Norwich
NR3 1YX

The ITIL series is available in a range of formats: hard copy, CD-ROM and now available as an Online Subscription. For further details and to purchase visit **www.get-best-practice.co.uk**

Any further enquiries or questions about ITIL or the Office of Government Commerce should be directed to the OGC Service Desk:

The OGC Service Desk
Rosebery Court
St Andrews Business Park
Norwich
NR7 0HS

Email: ServiceDesk@ogc.gsi.gov.uk
Telephone: 0845 000 4999

TSO will not sell, rent or pass any of your details onto interested third parties. The details you supply will be used for market research purposes only and to keep you up to date with TSO products and services which we feel maybe of interest to you. **If you would like us to use your information to keep you updated please indicate how you would like us to communicate with you:**

Telephone ☐   Email ☐   Mail ☐